(continued from previous page)

"Your books have saved my GPA, and quite possibly my sanity. My course grade is now an 'A', and I couldn't be happier."

Student, Winchester, IN

"These books are the best review books on the market. They are fantastic!"

Student, New Orleans, LA

"Your book was responsible for my success on the exam. . . I will look for REA the next time I need help."

Student, Chesterfield, MO

"I think it is the greatest study guide I have ever used!"

Student, Anchorage, AK

"I encourage others to buy REA because of their superiority. Please continue to produce the best quality books on the market."

Student, San Jose, CA

"Just a short note to say thanks for the great support your book gave me in helping me pass the test . . . I'm on my way to a B.S. degree because of you !"

Student, Orlando, FL

JAPANESE VERBS

P.M. Suski, Ph.D.
Professor of Japanese Language

and the Staff of
Research & Education Association,
Carl Fuchs, Language Program Director

Research & Education Association
61 Ethel Road West
Piscataway, New Jersey 08854

Dr. M. Fogiel, Director

SUPER REVIEW®
OF JAPANESE VERBS

Printed in the United States of America

Library of Congress Control Number 2001096033

International Standard Book Number 0-87891-423-4

SUPER REVIEW is a registered trademark of Research & Education Association, Piscataway, New Jersey 08854

WHAT THIS **Super Review**
WILL DO FOR YOU

This **Super Review** provides all that you need to know to do your homework effectively and succeed on exams and quizzes.

The book focuses on the core aspects of the subject, and helps you to grasp the important elements quickly and easily.

Outstanding **Super Review** features:

- Topics are covered in logical sequence

- Topics are reviewed in a concise and comprehensive manner

- The material is presented in student-friendly language that makes it easy to follow and understand

- Individual topics can be easily located

- Provides excellent preparation for midterms, finals and in-between quizzes

- Written by professionals and experts who function as your very own tutors

The key feature of this **Super Review** for learning Japanese Verbs is that it gives at a glance the person, mood and tense of the verbs—a priceless aid and time-saver to the student.

With the present book, the intricacies of learning the Japanese verbs are less formidable since all the verbs with their English equivalents are expressed in a clear and concise manner. As soon as the student understands the mechanical construction of the Japanese verbs, the student not only learns the language rapidly and without difficulty, but the verbs which had at first been intimidating become the most absorbingly interesting and fascinating branch of language study.

The challenge of preparing this book has been to present the different conjugations in so clear and intelligible a form that they could be readily comprehended, memorized and consulted by the average student who may not have had the time or inclination to review his or her grammar. By a properly directed study of the verbs one can, in a remarkably short period, not only learn to read and understand the language, but also be able to correctly speak, write and translate Japanese.

It is the function of this **Super Review** to help the student master the verbs with the minimum expenditure of time and effort. The student will learn to apply these verbs in practical conversation, becoming familiar not only with their usual grammatical significance, but also with their idiomatic use.

Dr. Max Fogiel, Program Director

Carl Fuchs, Chief Editor

CONTENTS

NOTE: The most common colloquial Japanese verbs defined in English, are given in lower section on every page except on pages 21, 28, 65 to 76.

For those who are used to Hepburn type of Romaji and not familiar with Romanized Kana or Japanese system of Romaji.

Read sha for sya	Read cha for tya	Read ja for dya or zya
Read shi for si	Read chi for ti	Read ji for di or zi
Read sho for syo	Read cho for tyo	Read jo for dyo or zyo
Read shu for syu	Read chu for tyu	Read ju for dyu or zyu
Read fu for hu	Read tsu for tu	Read dzu for du

Conjugation of Japanese Verbs

JAPANESE VERBS

In learning the Japanese language, perhaps no area poses a more difficult challenge for students than the Japanese verb endings. This book is a collection of the most popular Japanese verbs used in ordinary conversation, so that in a compact form the student can quickly see the most appropriate endings which are required in a given case. It is a priceless aid and time-saver to the student.

The challenge of preparing this book has been to present the different conjugations in so clear and intelligible a form that they could be readily comprehended, memorized and consulted by the average student who may not have had the time or inclination to review his or her grammar. Many of the polite forms and expressions which baffle beginners are treated rather extensively in tabulated form. By a properly directed study of the verbs one can, in a remarkably short period, not only learn to read and understand the language, but will be able to correctly speak, write and translate Japanese.

It is the function of this Super Review to help the student master the verbs with the minimum expenditure of time and effort. The student will learn to apply these verbs in practical conversation, becoming familiar not only with their usual grammatical significance, but also with their idiomatic use.

THE MOST COMMON JAPANESE VERBS DEFINED IN ENGLISH

The conjugation to which a verb belongs is indicated with a number. Abbreviations: ex., exo-active; en., endo-active; suff., suffix; syn., synonym; ct. exp., courteous expression; ob., obsolete.

Abaku (3 ex) to disclose; to disentomb; to break open; to expose; to reveal.

Abareru (7 en) to act violently, create disturbances.

Abiru (7 ex) to pour upon one's self, bathe.

Abiseru (7 ex) to pour over, throw over; to spatter.

Aburagiru (6 en) to be oily; to

Continued on next page (lower section)

The Romaji used to write Japanese words in this book is not the ordinary Romaji of Hepburn type, but it is the so-called Japanese system. The reason for this adoption is that the Japanese words written with this system can be readily converted into kana writing, while with the Hepburn system this can not be done properly at times. Kana written alphabetically is called Romanized kana, which is the same as those in the Japanese system.

THE ROMANIZED KANA

a	i	u	e	o
ka	ki	ku	ke	ko
sa	si	su	se	so
ta	ti	tu	te	to
na	ni	nu	ne	no
ha	hi	hu	he	ho
ma	mi	mu	me	mo
ya	—	yu	—	yo
ra	ri	ru	re	ro
wa	wi	—	we	wo
n				
ga	gi	gu	ge	go
za	zi	zu	ze	zo
da	di	du	de	do
ba	bi	bu	be	bo
pa	pi	pu	pe	po

The romanized kana is identical with the Japanese system of Romaji. There are as many syllables as there are kana characters; that is, 73. These syllables therefore are representative of Japanese kana characters in alphabetical writing, and not representative of Japanese kana sounds as is in case of Romaji of Hepburn.

To express combined kana sounds, the Japanese system of Romaji is used for the sake of uniformity.

The points of difference between the Japanese and ordinary or Hepburn system of Romaji are in the following 17 instances.

The Hepburn system spells: shi for si, chi for ti, tsu for tu, fu for hu, i for wi, e for we, ji for zi and di, zu for du, sha for sya, shu for syu, sho for syo, cha for tya, chu for tyu, cho for tyo, ja for zya and dya, ju for zyu and dyu, jo for zyo and dyo.

kya	—	kyu	—	kyo
sya	—	syu	—	syo
tya	—	tyu	—	tyo
nya	—	nyu	—	nyo
hya	—	hyu	—	hyo
mya	—	myu	—	myo
rya	—	ryu	—	ryo
gya	—	gyu	—	gyo
zya	—	zyu	—	zyo
dya	—	dyu	—	dyo
bya	—	byu	—	byo
pya	—	pyu	—	pyo

HOW THEY ARE PRONOUNCED

All vowels have the continental value, that is: a in sofa, i in ill, u in put, e in set, and o in obey. Consonants have sound value as in following examples: k in kite, s in so, t in top, n in now, h in hat, m in man, y in you, r in correct, w in was, g in get, z in zeal, d in dot, b in be, and p in pot. Insertion of y between a consonant and a vowel so modifies the consonant sound, as for example, from that of booty to beauty, or from cannon to canyon, etc.

For further details of Japanese pronunciation and Japanese writing systems, the readers are referred to pages 107—108 of this book.

Prolonged sounds of a, u or o are effected by addition of h after the vowel, thus: ah, uh, oh. When a vowel or y comes directly after

---

JAPANESE VERBS DEFINED IN ENGLISH
Continued from previous page (lower section)

be greasy.

Abureru (7 en) to return without profit.

Aburu (6 ex) to roast, bake, broil, toast; to warm.

Aeru (7 ex) to mix; to stir up.

Continued on next page (lower section)

such h in the same word, a hyphen is used between the h and the vowel or y, in order to avoid the error of combining in sound. Sounds of i or e are made long by addition of i, thus: ii or ei.

VERBS CLASSIFIED ACCORDING TO ENDINGS

All Japanese verbs are classified here according to the endings. There are eleven conjugations as we have eleven different endings. All Japanese verbs invariably end in u. The consonant which precedes the final u determines the conjugation. The vowel just before the final syllable is called the stem vowel of the verb. The stem vowel does not undergo change in conjugation except in the eleventh, which involves three different ways of changes.

The table appended gives principal endings of all conjugations. The present tense of indicative mood ends in bu, gu, ku, mu, nu, ru, su, tu, or u. The corresponding negative ends in ban, gan, kan, man, nan, ran, n, san, tan, wan, an. Past tense ends in nda, ida, ita, tta, ta, sita, or hta. Future tense ends in boh, goh, koh, moh, noh, roh, yoh, soh, toh, oh, oyoh, or iyoh. The imperative mood positive ends in be, ge, ke, me, ne, re, se, yo, te, e, oi, or ei. Connective mood is the form to which endings are attached or another verb may be connected to form a compound verb. The verbal noun is in the same form and ends in bi, gi, ki, mi, ni, ri, si, ti, or i.

Capital letters in the table indicate the stem vowels of verbs. The second, third, fourth, and sixth conjugations contain all five stem vowels, the eighth and tenth four, the first and ninth three, the seventh two, and the fifth has only one.

The verbs of seventh conjugation end in ru as those of sixth, but they have many peculiarities as follows; (1). Negative ends in single n. (2). Future and imperative are formed by substituting y in place of consonant in the ending syllable. (3). Connective and verbal noun are made by simply dropping off the ending.

All derivative verbs of any conjugation, such as passive, potential, compulsive, compulsive passive, compulsive potential, exo-active verbs and all modifications thereof end in eru and come under the seventh conjugation, although some of the exo-active verbs end in su.

JAPANESE VERBS DEFINED IN ENGLISH
Continued from previous page (lower section)

Agaku (3 en) to paw; to struggle.

Agameru (6 ex) to exalt, revere, worship.

Aganau (10 ex) to purchase, procure; to pay, to indemnify.

Agaru (6 en) to go up, ascend; to advance; to call or visit.

Agaru (6 ex) to eat or drink.

Ageru (7 ex) to raise, lift; to give; to mention; to fry.

Agumu (4 en) to be weary.

Ahureru (7 ex) to overflow, flood.

Aihansuru (11b en) to oppose to each other.

Aisuru (11b ex) to love, favor, be fond of.

Akaramu (4 en) to redden; to ripen; to blush; to grow red.

Akasu (8 ex) to disclose, reveal; to sit up all night; to satiate.

Akeharau (10 ex) to vacate.

Akeru (7 ex) to open; to empty; to vacate.

Akeru (7 en) to dawn.

Akinau (10 ex) to sell; to trade in.

Continued on next page (lower section)

TABLE OF BASIC CONJUGATIONS

Conjugation	1	2	3	4	5	6
Stem vowels	AEO	AEIOU	AEIOU	AEIOU	I	AEIOU
Present	bu	gu	ku	mu	nu	ru
Negative	ban	gan	kan	man	nan	ran
Past	nda	ida	ita	nda	nda	tta
Future	boh	goh	koh	moh	noh	roh
Imperative	be	ge	ke	me	ne	re
Connective) Substantive)	bi	gi	ki	mi	ni	ri
Examples	erabu	aogu	kaku	amu	sinu	soru

Conjugation	7	8	9	10	11a	11b	11c
Stem vowels	EI	AEOU	AOU	AIOU	U (changeable)		
Present	ru	su	tu	u	Uru	Uru	Uru
Negative	n	san	tan	wan	On	En	An
Past	ta	sita	tta	tta hta	Ita	Ita	nda
Future	yoh	soh	toh	oh	Oyoh	Iyoh	Oh
Imperative	yo	se	te	e	Oi	Ei	Ei
Connective) Substantive)	....	si	ti	i	I	I	I
Examples	ageru	osu	matu	arau	kuru	suru	inuru

JAPANESE VERBS DEFINED IN ENGLISH
Continued from previous page (lower section)

Akirameru (7 ex) to abandon the desire; to resign one's self to.

Akireru (7 en) to be astonished; to be amazed; to be dumbfounded.

Akiru (7 ex) to have enough of; to get tired of; to grow weary of. Syn. **Aku.**

Akitaru (6 en) to have enough of, be sated with.

Continued on next page (lower section)

REMARKS: Nearly thirty per cent of all verbs belong to the 7th conjugation, and twenty-five per cent to the 6th. Verbs of both of these conjugations end in ru, thereby making more than half of all Japanese verbs end in ru. Roughly about ten per cent each belong to 3rd, 4th, 8th and 10th conjugations. Between two and three per cent each belong to the 1st, 2nd and 9th conjugations. There are only one verb each to 5th, 11a, 11b and 11c, although 11b may serve as suffix to all nominal verbs, which must be distinguished from verbal nouns. Nominal verbs are usually composed of two or rarely one kanji or Chinese characters primarily serving as nouns signifying certain action, while a verbal noun is a noun directly derived from a verb.

As to the examples of verbs after each conjugation, all or nearly all verbs are given in cases of 1st, 2nd, 5th, 9th, 11a, 11b and 11c conjugations. But in cases of other conjugations the verbs are so numerous that only a part is given.

In English language the transitive verbs are defined as those which take direct object to complete the sense, and the intransitive verbs do not generally take direct object; in fact, the distinction between transitive and intransitive use of verbs is generally based on the presence or absence of the direct object word. Many Japanese verbs belonging to the intransitive class can and often do take the direct object word. It is therefore thought more convenient and clear to adopt the terms "exo-active" and "endo-active" for transitive and intransitive respectively in case of Japanese verbs.

An "exo-active" verb is a verb whose action or state directly involves a thing or person other than the subject. An "endo-active" verb is a verb whose action or state directly involves only the subject of the verb.

English grammar decrees that intransitive verbs have no passive form. But Japanese "endo-active" verbs have usually a corresponding passive form. For example: such expressions as "He is died by his wife.", "A police is escaped by his captive.", "A house is stepped in by a stranger," are in Japanese language, not only permissible, but are usually more excellent than a direct assertion in a colloquial speech.

There is no analogy of reflexive verbs in Japanese. Those verbs which are reflexive in English, are in Japanese a simple endo-active verb.

An "impersonal" verb is a classification which is entirely unnecessary in Japanese grammar. Really there is no such verb exactly corresponding to English "it snows," "it rains," "it hails," or "it thun-

---

JAPANESE VERBS DEFINED IN ENGLISH

Continued from previous page (lower section)

Akogareru (7 en) to be entranced; to be thrown into ecstacies; to long for, yearn after; to be infatuated with; to be absent-minded.

Aku (3 en) to open; to commence; to become empty; to come to end, (also same as **Akiru**).

Amaeru (7 en) to behave as a spoiled child; to take advantage of (one's kindness); to talk coquettishly.

Amanziru (7a en) see **Amanzuru**.

Amanzuru (7a or 11b en) to be contented, be satisfied.

Amaru (6 en) to remain; to be left over.

Amasu (8 ex) to leave over; to leave behind.

Amayakasu (8 ex) to pet, cod-

Continued on next page (lower section)

ders." Japanese expressions for those are analogous to "the snow falls," "the hail falls," "the thunder rolls."

Just as some of the English verbs may be transitive or intransitive according to the sense in which it is used; it is the same way in Japanese language. Very often the same one verb may be an exo-active or endo-active according to the way of thinking. Again, there are many verbs which are usually or mostly used as an exo-active, and others which are chiefly used as an endo-active, while still others which are used freely in both ways. But one must not overlook the fact that in many instances if a verb is used as an endo-active in Japanese, the corresponding English verb is usually employed as a transitive (analogous to exo-active) and vice versa. It also happens that with a verb of same sense, it may be used passively in Japanese, while in English it is used actively, and vice versa.

All these things are governed by the usage of the language, the knowledge of which is very important in acquirement of any foreign language, especially so with the Japanese which is so different in construction from the English in many respects.

Japanese verbs classed as "nominal verbs" given in the list later, are directly derived from Chinese characters. It is really a noun, denoting a verbal action or state, but it may be converted into a verb by suffixing a verb SURU (to do). Such verbs may be either an exo-active or endo-active. By using other suffixes, namely, -SARERU, -SIERU, -SASERU, -SASERARERU, etc. any verb of this class may be converted into passive, potential, compulsive, or compulsive-passive, forms.

COMPLETE CONJUGATIONS

In the following pages, complete conjugations are given in order from first to eleventh. The conjugation marked (a) gives the basic or primary conjugation with the meaning in English. The conjugation marked (b) gives the full conjugation covering under the class or part I the basic or primary expressions, under the part II the courteous expressions having chiefly the first and third persons as the subject of the verb and in first and second degrees of courteousness, and under the part III the courteous expressions in different degree having chiefly the second person as the subject.

The modes and tenses are: Indicative mode includes present, past, future and futurepast tenses, in positive and negative expressions; conditional mode in present, past and future, in positive and

---

JAPANESE VERBS DEFINED IN ENGLISH
Continued from previous page (lower section)

dle, spoil.

Amiau (10 en) to intertwine.

Amiawasu (8 ex) to interknit, intertwine.

Amidasu (8 ex) to work out, plan, devise, contrive.

Amu (8 ex) to net, knit, weave, mat, crochet.

Anadoru (6 ex) to disdain, despise; to look with scorn.

Anziru (7 ex) to think, feel uneasy about, plan, hold, grasp.

Aobamu (4 en) to grow green.

Aogu (2 ex) to fan.

Aogu (2 en) to look up, turn up, respect; to fan.

Aomuku (3 en) to look upward; to turn up.

Aoru (6 ex) to fan, incite, instigate, flap.

Continued on next page (lower section)

6

negative; imperative, adjectival and conjunctive modes in positive and negative; and connective and substantive modes in positive only.

The indicative mode is used for simple assertion; conditional mode implies probability or supposition; imperative mode for request or command; adjectival mode being verbal adjective to precede a noun; conjunctive mode includes the meaning of a conjunction "and" after a simple assertion; connective mode to connect another verb, suffix or a noun; substantive mode, being a verbal noun serves as a noun.

COURTEOUS MODES OF EXPRESSION

Part I (all persons). I, we, you, he, she, it or they, that is, all persons are used in connection with this class of verb. It is chiefly employed among persons of equal rank, with certain degree of intimacy, such as between students, comrades, etc., and is confined usually to conversation among male sex. Pronouns most often used in connection with verbs of this class are:

ore, wasi, watasi, boku, etc.	for I
wareware	for we
kisama, sonata, omae, kimi, etc.	for you
are	for he, she, it, or they
sore	for it, that, or they
dore	for which?
dare	for who?
nani	for what?

Part II (first and third persons). The subject of the verb in this class or part comprises I, we, he, she, it, they or person or persons on the speaker's side or rank, or sometimes the second person, especially when the verb is in an interrogative form. This is the usual style among women, and also among people not well acquainted or intimate with one another. The second degree of politeness in this class implies the object of the verb to be the second person. It naturally follows that endo-active verbs have the first degree of politeness only.

Part III. (second person). The subject of verbs in this class comprises: you, he, she, or they on the side of the person spoken to, or person or persons of same or higher rank. This form of verb is used when the action of verb refers to person addressed, any member of his family, his relatives, teachers, masters, employers, or persons in high station or nobility. The grades of politeness in expression are

---

JAPANESE VERBS DEFINED IN ENGLISH
Continued from previous page (lower section)

Aozameru (7 en) to pale, blanch; to turn white.

Arabiru (7 en) to be rough, violent or rowdy; to make a row.

Aradateru (7 ex) to excite; to agitate; to inflame; to aggravate.

Araitateru (7 ex) to rake up; to make an inquiry into.

Arakeru (7 ex) to stir up; to make separate.

Arakureru (7 ex) to become rowdy.

Ararageru (7 ex) to roughen; to make harsh (voice).

Arasou (10 en) to compete; to contend with, vie with; to quarrel with.

Arasu (8 ex) to ravage; to disturb; to pillage, loot.

Aratamaru (6 en) to change, renew; to improve.

Aratameru (7 ex) to correct; to

Continued on next page (lower section)

indicated with numbers 1, 2 or 3. When there is any appreciable distance in ranks of persons engaged in conversation, such as between employer and servants, customer and merchants, officers and enlistees, etc., it is customary for those in higher rank to use ordinary forms of class I and those on lower rank to use courteous forms of class II and III. Of course, persons on higher side may use courteous forms toward inferiors, in which case, the latter naturally seek to speak with higher degree of courteousness. Expressions of first, second, and third degree of politeness in classes II and III may be employed mixed, but the forms in class I should never be mixed in conversation with classes II and III, except in case of quotations.

The prefix o- attached to verbs in the second degree of politeness in class II and all in class III seems to show the subject or object of the verb is the second person. Therefore o- may be regarded to be a prefix of courteousness.

Proper forms of verbs according to ranks being provided as above stated, very often it is not necessary to express pronouns. When it is required for the sake of clearness to express pronouns in courteous speech, the following are most appropriate.

courteous	ordinary	meaning
watakusi	ore, etc.	I
watakusidomo	wareware	we
anata)		
anatasama)	kisama, etc.	you
kono-okata	kore	he, she
ano-kata	are	he, she
donata)		
donatasama)	dare	who?
dotirasama	dotira	which person?

ABBREVIATIONS

Abbreviations used in the tables of conjugations are as the following:

pres.	present
pas.	past
fut.	future
pos.	positive
neg.	negative

JAPANESE VERBS DEFINED IN ENGLISH

Continued from previous page (lower section)

revise; to rectify; to amend, mend.

Arau (10 ex) to rinse; to wash; to scour.

Arawareru (7 en) to come out, appear; to arise.

Arawasu (8 ex) to evince; to betray; to manifest; to open, expose, show; to write (a book); to compose.

Arehateru (7 en) to be desolate; to be waste; to be delapidated.

Aremawaru (6 en) to rush about; to storm about.

Areru (7 en) to run to waste; to be desolate; to be rowdy; to be stormy.

Ariamaru (6 en) to be superabundant; to overflow; to be in excess.

Arituku (3 en) to get; to find;

Continued on next page (lower section)

Mount Fuji

Confucian Temple

FIRST CONJUGATION (a)

INDICATIVE

pres. pos.	erabu	select
pres. neg.	eraban	select not
pas. pos.	eranda	did select
pas. neg.	erabananda	did not select
fut. pos.	eraboh	will select
fut. neg.	erabumai	will not have selected
fut. pas. pos.	erandaroh	will have selected
fut. pas. neg.	erabanandaroh	will not select

CONDITIONAL

pres. pos.	erabeba	if selects
pres. neg.	erabaneba	if does not select
pas. pos.	erandara	if did select
pas. neg.	erabanandaraba	if did not select
fut. pos.	erabohnaraba	if would select
fut. neg.	erabumainaraba	if would not select

IMPERATIVE

pos.	erabe	do select!
neg.	erabuna	do not select!

ADJECTIVAL

pos.	erabu	selecting
neg.	erabanu	not selecting

CONJUNCTIVE

pos.	erande	select and
neg.	erabanaide	select not and

CONNECTIVE

	erabi-	-----------------------

SUBSTANTIVE

	erabi	selection

INTERROGATIVE

JAPANESE VERBS DEFINED IN ENGLISH
Continued from previous page (lower section)

to come upon.

Ariuru (7a en) may be; can be; to be possible.

Aru (6 en) to be; there is; exist; occur; to lie, stand; to take place; to be performed.

Arukasu (8 ex) to make one walk.

Arukimawaru (6 en) to walk around, walk about, rove, wander.

Aruku (3 en) to walk; to go on foot. Syn. **Ayumu.**

Asariaruku (3 en) to prowl.

Asaru (6 ex) to fish for; to search for; to look for.

Asebamu (4 en) to sweat, perspire.

Aseru (6 en) to struggle; to scramble; to hurry; to grow impatient; to fade.

Continued on next page (lower section)

FIRST CONJUGATION (b)

	PART I. (all persons)	PART II. (1st and 3rd persons)	PART III. (2nd person)
INDICATIVE			
pres. pos.	erábu	1. erabimasu 2. oerabiitasimasu 2. oerabimohsimasu	1. oerabinasaru 1. Oerabininaru 2. oerabinasaimasu 2. oerabininarimasu 2. oerabiasobasu 3. oerabiasobasimasu
pres. neg.	eraban (ai)	1. erabimasen 2. oerabiitasimasen 2. oerabimohsimasen	1. oerabinasaran (ai) 1. oerabininaran (ai) 2. oerabinasaimasen 2. oerabininarimasen 2. oerabiasobasan (ai) 3. oerabiasobasimasen
pas. pos.	eranda	1. erabimasita 2. oerabiitasimasita 2. oerabimohsimasita	1. oerabinasatta 1. oerabininatta 2. oerabinasaimasita 2. oerabininarimasita 2. oerabiasobasita 3. oerabiasobasimasita
pas. neg.	erabananda erabanakatta	1. erabimasendesita 2. oerabiitasimasendesita 2. oerabimohsimasendesita	1. oerabinasarananda 1. oerabinasaranakatta 1. oerabininarananda 1. oerabininaranakatta 2. oerabinasaimasendesita 2. oerabininarimasendesita 2. oerabiasobasananda 2. oerabiasobasanakatta 3. oerabiasobasimasendesita
fut. pos.	eraboh	1. erabimasyoh 2. oerabiitasimasyoh 2. oerabimohsimasyoh	1. oerabinasaroh 1. oerabininaroh 2. oerabinasaimasyoh 2. oerabininarimasyoh 3. oerabiasobasimasyoh
		(-taroh or -tadesyoh, alternative)	
fut. neg.	erabumai	1. erabimasumai 2. oerabiitasimasumai 2. oerabimohsimasumai	1. oerabinasarumai 1. oerabininarumai 2. oerabinasaimasumai 2. oerabininarimasumai 2. oerabiasobasumai 3. oerabiasobasimasumai
		(-daroh or -dadesyoh, alternative)	
fut. pas. pos.	erandaroh	1. erabimasitaroh 2. oerabiitasimasitaroh 2. oerabimohsimasitaroh	1. oerabinasattaroh 1. oerabininattaroh 2. oerabinasaimasitaroh 2. oerabininarimasitaroh 3. oerabiasobasimasitaroh

---

JAPANESE VERBS DEFINED IN ENGLISH
Continued from previous page (lower section)

Asirau (10 ex) to receive; to treat; to handle; to serve.

Asobasu (8 ex) I. to make play; to let one be idle; II. (verb-ending of ct. exp.) to be pleased to.

Asobikurasu (8 en) to loaf; to idle away; to drone away.

Asobitawamureru (7 en) to dis-port; to sport; to gambol.

Asobu (1 en) to take a stroll; to be idle; to play.

Assuru (11b ex) to p r e s s, squeeze; to oppress; to crush.

Ataeru (7 ex) to give; to present; to donate; to bestow; to award.

Continued on next page (lower section)

erabanandaroh
    erabanakattaroh
    1. erabimasendesitaroh
    2. oerabiitasimasendesitaroh
    2. oerabimohsimasendesitaroh

1. oerabinasaranandaroh
1. oerabinasaranakattaroh
1. oerabininaranandaroh
1. oerabininaranakattaroh
2. oerabinasaimasendesitaroh
2. oerabininarimasendesitaroh
2. oerabiasobasanandaroh
2. oerabiasobasanakattaroh
3. oerabiasobasimasendesitaroh

CONDITIONAL
pres. pos. erabeba
    1. erabimasureba
    2. oerabiitasimasureba
    2. oerabimohsimasureba

1. oerabinasareba
1. oerabininareba
2. oerabinasaimasureba
2. oerabininarimasureba
2. oerabiasobaseba
3. oerabiasobasimasureba

pres. neg. erabaneba
    1. erabimasenkereba
    2. oerabiitasimaseneba
    2. oerabimohsimaseneba

1. oerabinasaraneba
1. oerabininaraneba
1. oerabininarankereba
2. oerabinasaimaseneba
2. oerabininarimasenkereba
2. oerabiasobasaneba
3. oerabiasobasimasenkereba

(-seneba or -senkereba, alternative)

pas. pos. erandara(ba)
    1. erabimasitara(ba)
    2. oerabiitasimasitara(ba)
    2. oerabimohsimasitara(ba)

1. oerabinasattara(ba)
1. oerabininattara(ba)
2. oerabinasaimasitara(ba)
2. oerabininarimasitara(ba)
2. oerabiasobasitara(ba)
3. oerabiasobasimasitara(ba)

pas. neg. erabanandara(ba)
    1. erabimasendesitara(ba)
    2. oerabiitasimasendesitara(ba)
    2. oerabimohsimasendesitara(ba)

1. oerabinasaranandara(ba)
1. oerabinasaranakattara(ba)
1. oerabininaranandara(ba)
1. oerabininaranakattara(ba)
2. oerabinasaimasendesitara(ba)
2. oerabininarimasendesitara(ba)
2. oerabiasobasanandara(ba)
2. oerabiasobasanakattara(ba)
3. oerbaiasobasimasendesitara(ba)

fut. pos. erabohnara(ba)
    1. erabimasyohnara(ba)
    2. oerabiitasimasyohnara(ba)
    2. oerabimohsimasyohnara(ba)

1. oerabinasarohnara(ba)
1. oerabininarohnara(ba)
2. oerabinasaimasyohnara(ba)
2. oerabininarimasyohnara(ba)
2. oerabiasobasohnara(ba)
3. oerabiasobasimasyohnara(ba)

fut. neg. erabumainara(ba)
    1. erabimasumainara(ba)
    2. oerabiitasimasumainara(ba)
    2. oerabimohsimasumainara(ba)

1. oerabinasarumainara(ba)
1. oerabininarumainara(ba)
2. oerabinasaimasumainara(ba)
2. oerabininarimasumainara(ba)
2. oerabiasobasumainara(ba)
3. oerabiasobasimasumainara(ba)

JAPANESE VERBS DEFINED IN ENGLISH
Continued from previous page (lower section)

Atarasigaru (6 en) to believe oneself to be up-to-date; to believe to be new.

Ataritirasu (8 en) to vent one's anger at random.

Ataru (6 en) to correspond to; to hit the mark; to knock against; to meet; to fall on; to come out right; to succeed; to be exposed to.

Atatamaru (6 en) to become warm; to warm oneself.

Atatameru (7 ex) to warm; to cherish.

Atattemiru (7 ex) to dare; to sound; to probe.

Atau (10 en) to be able to; can.

Ategau (10 ex) to allot, assign; to appropriate; to provide.

Atehamaru (6 en) to be applic-

Continued on next page (lower section)

IMPERATIVE (addressed to the 2d person only)

pos.	erabe		1. oerabinasai
			2. oerabinasaimase
			2. oerabiasobase
			3. oerabiasobasimase
neg.	erabuna		1. oerabinasaruna
			2. oerabinasaimasuna
			2. oerabiasobasuna
			3. oerabiasobasimasuna

ADJECTIVE

pos.	erabu	1. erabimasu(ru)	1. oerabinasaru
		2. oerabiitasimasu(ru)	1. oerabininaru
		2. oerabimohsimasu(ru)	2. oerabinasaimasu(ru)
			2. oerabininarimasu(ru)
			2. oerabiasobasu
			3. oerabiasobasimasu(ru)
neg.	eraban(u)	1. erabimasen(u)	1. oerabinasaran(u)(ai)
	erabanai	2. oerabiitasimasen(u)	1. oerabininaran(u)(ai)
		2. oerabimohsimasen(u)	2. oerabinasaimasen(u)
			2. oerabininarimasen(u)
			2. oerabiasobasan(u)(ai)
			3. oerabiasobasimasen(u)

CONJUNCTIVE

pos.	erande	1. erabimasite	1. oerabinasatte
		2. oerabiitasimasite	1. oerabininatte
		2. oerabimohsimasite	2. oerabinasaimasite
			2. oerabininarimasite
			2. oerabiasobasite
			3. oerabiasobasimasite
neg.	erabande	1. erabimasende(site)	1. oerabinasaranaide
	erabanaide	2. oerabiitasimasende(site)	1. oerabininaranaide
	erabanukutte	2. oerabimohsimasende(site)	2. oerabinasaimasende(site)
			2. oerabininarimasende(site)
			2. oerabiasobasanaide
			3. oerabiasobasimasende(site)

(-naide or -nakutte, alternative)

CONNECTIVE

erabi-

SUBJUNCTIVE

erabi

INTERROGATIVE:

By suffixing -ka, all verbs in classes I. II, III of indicative mode may be converted into interrogative. Conditional, imperative, adjective, connective and substantive modes have no interrogative forms.

JAPANESE VERBS DEFINED IN ENGLISH
Continued from previous page (lower section)

able; to fit, suit; to be pertinent.

Atehameru (7 ex) to apply; to fit; to frame; to shape; to adapt, adjust.

Atekosuru (6 en) to hint at; to hint a fault; to imply rebuke.

Aterareru (7 en) to be guessed right; to be poisoned by; to be affected by; to be tortured.

Ateru (7 ex) to apply; to hit; to touch; to assign; to address; to direct.

Atodukeru (7 en) to trace; to follow.

Atohiku (3 en) to trail.

Atukau (10 ex) to handle, manage; to deal with; to mediate; to use; to treat.

Atumaru (6 en) to gather together, collect, flock, swarm; to

Continued on next page (lower section)

All verbs in conditional and conjunctive modes, as well as those of indicative mode as above may be used interrogatively by rising inflection of the last syllable in pronunciation.

REMARKS: Final syllables enclosed in brackets as (ai), (ru), (u), (ba) and (site) are optional. That is: they may be dispensed with or used so attached. It is usually somewhat more polite if these final syllables are appended.

It is optional to use either one of endings indicated thus: (-taroh or -tadesyoh), (-daroh or -dadesyoh), (-naide or -nakutte). It is slightly more polite to use -tadesyoh, -dadesyoh in place of -taroh, -daroh. There is hardly any difference between -naide and -nakutte.

The prefix of courteousness o- is used before all Japanese verbs in Japanese sounds; 1. when the action of the verb is attributed to the second person or the person addressed and respected, and, 2. when the action is by the speaker and for the person addressed. Other prefixes of courteousness are: go-, gyo-, mi-, on-, etc., among which go- is often used with nominal verbs of two characters, but the rest are not heard in colloquial Japanese, except in quotations. See further under the nominal verbs.

These remarks apply to all conjugations.

THE VERBS OF THE FIRST CONJUGATION

Exo-active verbs	Endo-active verbs
erabu, to select, to choose.	narabu, to be in line.
manabu, to study, to learn.	sakebu, to cry.
musubu, to tie, to unite.	musebu, to be choked.
yobu, to call.	asobu, to play.
tattobu, to venerate.	korobu, to fall down.
tohtobu, to venerate.	horobu, to perish.
moteasobu, to play with.	sinobu, to bear.
	tobu, to jump, to fly.
	hokorobu, to rip.
	yorokobu, to be glad.

The above is nearly all the simple verbs of this conjugation. Compound verbs with another element preceding, such as **torimusubu**, **nakisakebu**, **taesinobu**, etc., also belong to this conjugation. Exo-active verbs generally take full conjugation. Endo-active verbs are not conjugated in 2d degree polite form of class II. Same is true with some exo-active verbs which cannot have the second person as direct object; for example, **manabu**.

Some impersonal verbs as **horobu** or **hokorobu** are not conjugated entirely in class III and in 2d degree polite form of class II. **Tattobu**, **tohtobu** and **moteasobu** also come under this group. Therefore these verbs seldom take the prefix of courteousness o-.

Such verbs as **yobu, tobu, tattobu, tohtobu**, etc., are rarely used in substantive mode.

JAPANESE VERBS DEFINED IN ENGLISH
Continued from previous page (lower section)

crowd; to meet, assemble.

    Atumeru (7 ex) to collect, gather, assemble; to compile.

    Aturaeru (7 ex) to order; to be-

speak.

    Au (10 en) to agree, accord, fit, suit; to become; to pay; to meet; to come across, encounter, chance

Continued on next page (lower section)

THE SECOND CONJUGATION (a)

INDICATIVE

pres. pos.	aogu	fan
pres. neg.	aogan	fan not
past pos.	aoida	did fan
past neg.	aogananda	did not fan.
fut. pos.	aogoh	will fan.
fut. neg.	aogumai	will not fan.
fut. past pos.	aoidaroh	will have fanned.
fut. past neg.	aoganandaroh	will not have fanned.

CONDITIONAL

pres. pos.	aogeba	if fans
pres. neg.	aoganeba	if does not fan
past pos.	aoidara	if did fan
past neg.	aoganandara	if did not fan
fut. pos.	aogohnaraba	if would fan
fut. neg.	aogumainaraba	if would not fan

IMPERATIVE

pos.	aoge	do fan!
neg.	aoguna	do not fan!

ADJECTIVAL

pos.	aogu	fanning
neg.	aoganu	not fanning

CONJUNCTIVE

pos.	aoide	fan and
neg.	aoganaide	fan not and

CONNECTIVE

	aogi	....

SUBSTANTIVE

	aogi	fanning

INTERROGATIVE

JAPANESE VERBS DEFINED IN ENGLISH
Continued from previous page (lower section)

upon, meet with, fall in with.

Awadatu (9 en) to foam, froth; to bubble, effervesce.

Awaremu (4 ex) to pity, sympathize, compassionate, feel sorry for.

Awaseru (7 ex) to unite, combine, join together; to match; to put together; to add; to mix; to arrange; to bring together.

Awateru (7 en) to be confused, be agitated, be flustered.

Ayabumu (4 en) to be afraid of; to apprehend; to fear; to doubt.

Ayakaru (6 en) to resemble; to take after.

Ayamaru (6 en) to mistake; to make an error; to apologize.

Ayamaru (6 ex) to mislead; to mismanage; to miss.

Ayamatu (9 en) to make an

Continued on next page (lower section)
14

THE SECOND CONJUGATION (b)

	I (all persons)	II (1st and 3d persons)	III (2d person)
INDICATIVE			
pres. pos.	aogu	1. aogimasu 2. oaogiitasimasu 2. oaogimohsimasu	1. oaoginasaru 1. oaogininaru 2. oaoginasaimasu 2. oaogininarimasu 2. oaogiasobasu 3. oaogiasobasimasu
pres. neg.	aogan(ai)	1. aogimasen 2. oaogiitasimasen 2. oaogimohsimasen	1. oaoginasaran(ai) 1. oaogininaran(ai) 2. oaoginasaimasen 2. oaogininarimasen 2. oaogiasobasan(ai) 3. oaogiasobasimasen
pas. pos.	aoida	1. aogimasita 2. oaogiitasimasita 2. oaogimohsimasita	1. oaoginasatta 1. oaogininatta 2. oaoginasaimasita 2. oaogininarimasita 2. oaogiasobasita 3. oaogiasobasimasita
pas. neg.	aogananda aoganakatta	1. aogimasendesita 2. oaogiitasimasendesita 2. oaogimohsimasendesita	1. oaoginasarananda 1. oaoginasaranakatta 1. oaogininarananda 1. oaogininaranakatta 2. oaoginasaimasendesita 2. oaogininarimasendesita 2. oaogiasobasananda 2. oaogiasobasanakatta 3. oaogiasobasimasendesita
fut. pos.	aogoh	1. aogimasyoh 2. oaogiitasimasyoh 2. oaogimohsimasyoh	1. oaoginasaroh 1. oaogininaroh 2. oaoginasaimasyoh 2. oaogininarimasyoh 3. oaogiasobasimasyoh
fut. neg.	aogumai	1. aogimasumai 2. oaogiitasimasumai 2. oaogimohsimasumai	1. oaoginasarumai 1. oaogininarumai 2. oaoginasaimasumai 2. oaogininarimasumai 2. oaogiasobasumai 3. oaogiasobasimasumai
fut. pas. pos.	aoidaroh	1. aogimasitaroh 2. oaogimohsimasitadesyoh 2. oaogiitasimasitadesyoh	1. oaoginasattaroh 1. oaogininattaroh 2. oaoginasaimasitaroh 2. oaogininarimasitaroh 2. oaogiasobasitaroh 3. oaogiasobasimasitaroh
fut. pas. neg.	aoganandaroh aoganakattaroh 1. aogimasendesitaroh 2. oaogiitasimasendesitaroh 2. oaogimohsimasendesitaroh	1. oaoginasaranandaroh 1. oaoginasaranakattaroh 1. oaogininaranakattaroh 2. oaoginasaimasendesitaroh 2. oaogininarimasendesitaroh 2. oaogiasobasanakattaroh 3. oaogiasobasimasendesitaroh	

(-daroh or -dadesyoh,
-taroh or -tadesyoh), alternative

JAPANESE VERBS DEFINED IN ENGLISH

Continued from previous page (lower section)

error.

Ayameru (7 ex) to kill; to murder.

Ayanasu (8 ex) to play with; to make a puppet of.

Ayasimu (4 ex) to doubt; to suspect; to wonder.

Ayaturu (6 ex) to manage; to

Continued on next page (lower section)

CONDITIONAL

pres. pos. aogeba

1. aogimasureba
2. oagiitasimasureba
2. oaogimohsimasureba

1. oaoginasareba
1. oaogininareba
2. oaoginasaimasureba
2. oaogininarimasureba
2. oaogiasobaseba
3. oaogiasobasimasureba

pres. neg. aoganeba

1. aogimasenkereba
2. oaogiitasimaseneba
2. oaogimohsimaseneba
   (-seneba or senkereba)
   alternative

1. oaoginasaraneba
1. oaogininaraneba
2. oaoginasaimaseneba
2. oaogininarimaseneba
2. oaogiasobasaneba
3. oaogiasobasimasenkereba

pas. pos. aoidara(ba)

1. aogimasitara(ba)
2. oaogiitasimasitara(ba)
2. oaogimohsimasitara(ba)

1. oaoginasattara(ba)
1. oaogininattara(ba)
2. oaoginasaimasitara(ba)
2. oaogininarimasitara(ba)
2. oaogiasobasitara(ba)
3. oaogiasobasimasitara(ba)

pas. neg. aoganandara(ba)
aoganakattara(ba)

1. aogimasendesitara(ba)
2. oaogiitasimasendesitara(ba)
2. oaogimohsimasendesitara(ba)

1. oaoginasaranandara(ba)
1. oaoginasaranakattara(ba)
1. oaogininaranakattara(ba)
2. oaoginasaimasendesitara(ba)
2. oaogininarimasendesitara(ba)
2. oaogiasobasanandara(ba)
3. oaogiasobasimasendesitara(ba)

fut. pos. aogohnara(ba)

1. aogimasyohnara(ba)
2. oaogiitasimasyohnara(ba)
2. oaogimohsimasyohnara(ba)

1. oaoginasarohnara(ba)
1. oaogininarohnara(ba)
2. oaoginasaimasyohnara(ba)
2. oaogiasobasohnara(ba)
3. oaogiasobasimasyohnara(ba)

fut. neg. aogumainara(ba)

1. aogimasumainara(ba)
2. oaogiitasimasumainara(ba)
2. oaogimohsimasumainara(ba)

1. oaoginasarumainara(ba)
1. oaogininarumainara(ba)
2. oaoginasaimasumainara(ba)
2. oaogininarimasumainara(ba)
2. oaogiasobasumainara(ba)
3. oaogiasobasimasumainara(ba)

JAPANESE VERBS DEFINED IN ENGLISH
Continued from previous page (lower section)

work; to work a puppet; to manipulate.

Ayumu (4 en) to walk; to tread; to go on foot. Syn. Aruku.

Azakeru (6 ex) to scoff at, jeer at; to mock, scoff, sneer.

Azamuku (3 ex) to deceive, cheat; to defraud, impose upon.

Azawarau (10 ex) to sneer, ridicule; to laugh at, mock at.

Azukaru (6 ex) to keep; to have custody of; to take a thing in charge.

Azukaru (6 en) to take a part in; to participate in.

Azukeru (7 ex) to consign, give in charge; to entrust with; to deposit.

Bakasu (8 ex) to bewitch, enchant, cheat.

Bakeru (7 en) to take form of, transform into.

Bakusuru (11b ex) to attack, assault; to refute; to bind; to arrest.

-bamu (4 suff.) to be tinged with; to grow.

Barasu (8 ex) to expose; to kill.

Bareru (7 en) to be discovered; to come to light.

Bassuru (11b ex) to punish.

Benzuru (7a or 11b ex) to distinguish, discern; to transact; to accommodate.

Benzuru (7a or 11b en) to speak; to controvert.

Betatuku (3 en) to be sticky.

Bikutuku (3 en) to start, be afraid.

Bokeru (7 en) to grow mentally

Continued on next page (lower section)
16

Heian Jingu Shrine

Banrukun Rock Gardens

IMPERATIVE

pos.	aoge	....	1. oaoginasai
			2. oaoginasaimase
			2. oaogiasobase
			3. oaogiasobasimase

neg.	aoguna	....	1. oaoginasaruna
			2. oaoginasaimasuna
			2. oaogiasobasuna
			3. oaogiasobasimasuna

ADJECTIVAL

pos.	aogu	1. aogimasu(ru)	1. oaoginasaru
		2. oaogiitasimasu(ru)	1. oaogininaru
		2. oaogimohsimasu(ru)	2. oaoginasaimasu(ru)
			2. oaogininarimasu(ru)
			2. oaogiasobasu
			3. oaogiasobasimasu(ru)

neg.	aogan(u)	1. aogimasen(u)	1. oaoginasaran(u,ai)
	aoganai	2. oaogiitasimasen(u)	1. oaogininaran(u,ai)
		2. oaogimohsimasen(u)	2. oaoginasaimasen(u)
			2. oaogininarimasen(u)
			2. oaogiasobasan(u,ai)
			3. oaogiasobasimasen(u)

CONJUNCTIVE

pos.	aoide	1. aogimasite	1. oaoginasatte
		2. oaogiitasimasite	1. oaogininatte
		2. oaogimohsimasite	2. oaoginasaimasite
			2. oaogininarimasite
			2. oaogiasobasite
			3. oaogiasobasimasite

neg.	aoganaide	1. aogimasende(site)	1. oaoginasaranaide
	aogande	2. oaogiitasimasende(site)	1. oaogininaranaide
	aoganakutte	2. oaogimohsimasende(site)	2. oaoginasaimasende(site)
			2. oaogininarimasende(site)
			2. oaogiasobasanaide
			3. oaogiasobasimasende(site)

(-naide or -nakutte) alternative

CONNECTIVE
    aogi

SUBSTANTIVE
    aogi

INTERROGATIVE (see note under 1st conjugation)

JAPANESE VERBS DEFINED IN ENGLISH
Continued from previous page (lower section)

weak, be weak-minded; to fade.

Bokusuru (11b ex) to divine; to augur; to govern; to lead.

Boru (6 ex) to be greedy of; to over-charge.

Bossuru (11b en) to sink; to go down; to set (as moon or sun); to disappear; to die; to pass away.

Bukkakeru (7 ex) to dash over (as water).

Burasagaru (6 en) to hang; to dangle.

Buratuku (3 en) to wander about, saunter, ramble, stroll.

Buru (6 en) to affect, put on, pretend.

Butikowasu (8 ex) to smash, crash, destroy.

Buttukaru (6 en) to bump against, clash with, collide with.

Buttukeru (7 ex) to throw; to fling.

Dabutuku (3 en) to be loose; to splash.

Daku (3 ex) to embrace, hug.

Dakusuru (11b en) to consent, assent to.

Damaru (6 en) to shut up, hush up; to be silent.

Damasu (8 ex) to deceive, de-

Continued on next page (lower section)

17

THE VERBS OF THE SECOND CONJUGATION

Exo-active verbs

hagu, to strip off.
hisagu, to sell.
hisigu, to crush.
husagu, to block.
husegu, to prevent.
kagu, to smell.
kasegu, to earn.
kasigu, to cook.
katugu, to carry.
kogu, to row.
nugu, to take off.
oyogu, to swim.
sinogu, to bear.
sogu, to cut off.
sosogu, to pour over.

susugu, to rinse.
togu, to grind.
tugu, to join.
tumugu, to spin.
tunagu, to tie.

Endo-active verbs

aogu, to look up.
kasegu, to toil.
isogu, to hurry.
nagu, to calm.
sawagu, to make merry.
soyogu, to breeze.
totugu, to marry.
usuragu, to lighten.
yawaragu, to soften.

The above are nearly all of simple verbs belonging to the Second Conjugation. Compound verbs with these verbs as ending are possible and are of course conjugated according to the ending. Almost all exo-active verbs above take full conjugation. Some such verbs as **hisagu, hisigu, kagu, oyogu,** etc., are not usually conjugated in full in class II. Endo-active verbs also come under this category. Impersonal verbs as **nagu, soyogu, usuragu,** and **yawaragu** are not conjugated in class III entirely. A few verbs as **hagu, sogu,** etc., are not used in substantive mode, except in compounds.

The verb **aogu** as used in the full conjugation above is the exo-active verb, meaning to fan, while the verb of the same spelling meaning to look up is an endo-active verb, which is not to be fully conjugated. Other examples of exo- and endo-active verbs in the same spelling and conjugation are given below:

EXO- AND ENDO-ACTIVE VERBS IN SAME SPELLING

Akeru (7 ex) to open; (7 en) to dawn.
Husagu (2 ex) to close; (2 en) to be gloomy.
Huseru (7 ex) to cover; (6 en) to sleep.
Kagiru (6 ex) to limit; (6 en) to be limited.
Tumoru (6 ex) to estimate; (6 en) to accumulate.
Tumu (4 ex) to pluck; (4 en) to accumulate.
Tunoru (6 ex) to assemble; (6 en) to augment.
Ueru (7 ex) to plant; (7 en) to hunger.
Utikomu (4 ex) to knock in; (4 en) to be infatuated.
Wataru (6 ex) to wade; (6 en) to extend.

With the single exception of **Huseru** in above, the exo- and endo-active verbs take the same conjugation.

JAPANESE VERBS DEFINED IN ENGLISH

Continued from previous page (lower section)

fraud, cheat.
Danziru (7 en) to speak.
Danzuru (7a or 11b en) to

speak, say, talk.
Darakeru (7 en) to feel languid; to slacken; one's effort; to be idle.

Continued on next page (lower section)

18

THE THIRD CONJUGATION (a)

INDICATIVE
pres. pos.	kaku	write
pres. neg.	kakan	write not
pas. pos.	kaita	did write
pas. neg.	kakananda	did not write
fut. pos.	kakoh	will write
fut. neg.	kakumai	will not write
fut. pas. pos.	kaitaroh	will have written
fut. pas. neg.	kakanandaroh	will not have written

CONDITIONAL
pres. pos.	kakeba	if writes
pres. neg.	kakaneba	if does not write
pas. pos.	kaitara	if did write
pas. neg.	kakanandara	if did not write
fut. pos.	kakohnaraba	if would write
fut. neg.	kakumainaraba	if would not write

IMPERATIVE
pos.	kake	do write!
neg.	kakuna	do not write!

ADJECTIVAL
neg.	kaku	writing
neg.	kakanu	not writing

CONJUNCTIVE
pos.	kaite	write and
pos.	kakanaide	write not and

CONNECTIVE
	kaki	....

SUBSTANTIVE
	kaki	writing

INTERROGATIVE

JAPANESE VERBS DEFINED IN ENGLISH
Continued from previous page (lower section)

Dasinuku (3 en) to steal a march on.

Dasisiburu (6 en) to grudge; to be unwilling to pay.

Dassuru (11b ex) to leave out, omit; to cast off, shed; to take off; to escape from; to rise above of.

Dasu (8 ex) to put out; to put forth; to send out; to pull out; to protrude; to bring out; to publish; to produce; to exhibit; to discharge.

-dasu (8 suff.) to begin to - - -.

Deau (10 en) to encounter, meet with; to gather.

Debaru (6 en) to project, protrude.

Dekakeru (7 en) to start; to go

Continued on next page (lower section)

THE THIRD CONJUGATION (b)

PART I (all persons)	PART II (1st & 3rd persons)	PART III (2d person)
INDICATIVE		
pres pos. kaku	1. kakimasu 2. okakiitasimasu 2. okakimohsimasu	1. okakinasaru 1. okakininaru 2. okakinasaimasu 2. okakininarimasu 2. okakiasobasu 3. okakiasobasimasu
pres. neg. kakan(ai)	1. kakimasen 2. okakiitasimasen 2. okakimohsimasen	1. oakinasaran(ai) 1. okakininaran(ai) 2. okakinasaimasen 2. okakininarimasen 2. okakiasobasan(ai) 3. okakiasobasimasen
pas. pos. kaita	1. kakimasita 2. okakiitasimasita 2. okakimohsimasita	1. okakinasatta 1. okakininatta 2. okakinasaimasita 2. okakininarimasita 2. okakiasobasita 3. okakiasobasimasita
pas. neg. kakananda kakanakatta	1. kakimasendesita 2. okakiitasimasendesita 2. okakimohsimasendesita	1. okakinasarananda 1. okakinasaranakatta 1. okakininarananda 1. okakininaranakatta 2. okakinasaimasendesita 2. okakininarimasendesita 2. okakiasobasananda 2. okakiasobasanakatta 3. okakiasobasimasendesita
fut. pos. kakoh	1. kakimasyoh 2. okakiitasimasyoh 2. okakimohsimasyoh	1. okakinasaroh 1. okakininaroh 2 .okakinasaimasyoh 2. okakininarimasyoh 3. okakiasobasimasyoh
fut. neg. kakumai	1. kakimasumai 2. okakiitasimasumai 2. okakimohsimasumai	1. okakinasarumai 1. okakininarumai 2. okakinasaimasumai 2. okakininarimasumai 2. okakiasobasumai 3. okakiasobasimasumai
fut. pas. pos. kaitaroh	1. kakimasitaroh 2. okakiitasimasitaroh 2. okakimohsimasitaroh	1. okakinasattaroh 1. okakininattaroh 2. okakinasaimasitaroh 2. okakininarimasitaroh 2. okakiasobasitaroh 3. okakiasobasimasitadesyoh
fut. pas. neg. kakanandaroh kakanakattaroh	1. kakimasendesitaroh 2. okakiitasimasendesitaroh 2. okakimohsimasendesitaroh	1. okakinasaranandaroh 1. okakinasaranakattaroh 1. okakininaranandaroh 1. okakininaranakattaroh 2. okakinasaimasendesitaroh 2. okakininarimasendesitaroh 2. okakiasobasanandaroh 2. okakiasobasanakattaroh 3. okakiasobasimasendesitaroh

(-daroh or -dadesyoh, -taroh or -tadesyoh, alternative)

JAPANESE VERBS DEFINED IN ENGLISH
Continued from previous page (lower section)

out; to set out.
Dekasu (8 ex) to do; to bring to pass; to succeed; to complete.

Dekiru (7 en) to be able; to be in one's power; to be made; to be proficient, be skilled; to be finish-

Continued on page 22 lower section

CONDITIONAL

pres. pos.	kakeba	1. kakimasureba 2. okakiitasimasureba 2. okakimohsimasureba	1. okakinasareba 1. okakininareba 2. okakinasaimasureba 2. okakininarimasureba 2. okakiasobaseba 3. okakiasobasimasureba
pres. neg.	kakaneba	1. kakimasenkereba 2. okakiitasimaseneba 2. okakimohsimaseneba	1. okakinasaraneba 1. okakininaraneba 1. okakininarankereba 2. okakinasaimaseneba 2. okakininarimasenkereba 2. okakiasobasaneba 3. okakiasobasimasenkereba

(-seneba or -senkereba, alternative)

pas. pos.	kaitara(ba)	1. kakimasitara(ba) 2. okakiitasimasitara(ba) 2. okakimohsimasitara(ba)	1. okakinasattara(ba) 1. okakininattara(ba) 2. okakinasaimasitara(ba) 2. okakininarimasitara(ba) 2. okakiasobasitara(ba) 3. okakiasobasimasitara(ba)
pas. neg.	kakanandara(ba) kakanakattara(ba)	1. kakimasendesitara(ba) 2. okakiitasimasendesitara(ba) 2. okakimohsimasendesitara(ba)	1. okakinasaranandara(ba) 1. okakinasaranakattara(ba) 1. okakininaranandara(ba) 1. okakininaranakattara(ba) 2. okakinasaimasendesitara(ba) 2. okakininarimasendesitara(ba) 2. okakiasobasanandara(ba) 2. okakiasobasanakattara(ba) 3. okakiasobasimasendesitara(ba)
fut. pos.	kakohnara(ba)	1. kakimasyohnara(ba) 2. okakiitasimasyohnara(ba) 2. okakimohsimasyohnara(ba)	1. okakinasarohnara(ba) 1. okakininarohnara(ba) 2. okakinasaimasyohnara(ba) 2. okakininarimasyohnara(ba) 2. okakiasobasohnara(ba) 3. okakiasobasimasyohnara(ba)
fut. neg.	kakumainara(ba)	1. kakimasumainara(ba) 2. okakiitasimasumainara(ba) 2. okakimohsimasumainara(ba)	1. okakinasarumainara(ba) 1. okakininarumainara(ba) 2. okakinasaimasumainara(ba) 2. okakininarimasumainara(ba) 2. okakiasobasumainara(ba) 3. okakiasobasimasumainara(ba)

IMPERATIVE (addressed to second person only).

pos.	kake	1. okakinasai 2. okakinasaimase 2. okakiasobase 3. okakiasobasimase
neg.	kakuna	1. okakinasaruna 2. okakinasaimasuna 2. okakiasobasuna 3. okakiasobasimasuna

ADJECTIVE

pos.	kaku	1. kakimasu(ru) 2. okakiitasimasu(ru) 2. okakimohsimasu(ru)	1. okakinasaru 1. okakininaru 2. okakinasaimasu(ru) 2. okakininarimasu(ru) 2. okakiasobasu 3. okakiasobasimasu(ru)
neg.	kakan(u) kakanai	1. kakimasen(u) 2. okakiitasimasen(u) 2. okakimohsimasen(u)	1. okakinasaran(u)(ai) 1. okakininaran(u)(ai) 2. okakinasaimasen(u) 2. okakininarimasen(u) 2. okakiasobasan(u)(ai) 3. okakiasobasimasen(u)

21

pos.	kaite	1. kakimasite 2. okakiitasimasite 2. okakimohsimasite	1. okakinasatte 1. okakininatte 2. okakinasaimasite 2. okakininarimasite 2. okakiasobasite 3. okakiasobasimasite
neg.	kakande kakanaide kakanakutte	1. kakimasende(site) 2. okakiitasimasende(site) 2. okakimohsimasende(site)	1. okakinasaranaide 1. okakininaranaide 2. okakinasaimasende(site) 2. okakininarimasende(site) 2. okakiasobasanaide(site) 3. okakiasobasimasende(site)

(naide or nakutte, alternative)

CONNECTIVE
    kaki-
SUBSTANTIVE
    kaki

THE VERBS OF THE THIRD CONJUGATION

As there are about ten per cent of all Japanese verbs belonging to the third conjugation, the examples here are only a part of them.

Exo-active verbs	Endo-active verbs
daku, to hug.	hibiku, to resound.
hiku, to pull.	kawaku, to thirst.
kiku, to hear.	muku, to turn.
maneku, to beckon.	nageku, to lament.
muku, to peel.	odoroku, to wonder.
nozoku, to expel.	saku, to bloom.
oku, to put.	tuku, to adhere.
saku, to rend.	ugoku, to move.
toku, to untie.	ugomeku, to wriggle.
tuku, to thrust.	uku, to float.
yaku, to burn.	uzumaku, to whirl.

Among the above, there are three verbs which have the same form in the exo and endo-active. They are saku, tuku and muku. In actual speech, there is little chance for confusion, as saku, when meaning to rend is accented on the first syllable, while when meaning to bloom it is accented on the last. In the exo-active, tuku is accented on the last syllable, and in the endo-active, it is accented on the first. Muku is always accented on the last syllable.

JAPANESE VERBS DEFINED IN ENGLISH
Continued from page 20 lower section

ed; to be possible.

Dekuwasu (8 en) to happen on; to meet; to come across, chance upon.

Demuku (3 en) to go; to proceed.

Denaosu (8 en) to come again; to go out again.

Deru (7 en) to go out; to come out; to appear, to be produced; to be published; to start; to originate from.

Desugiru (7 en) to be too far out; to intrude upon; to be too

Continued on next page (lower section)

THE FOURTH CONJUGATION (a)

INDICATIVE

pres. pos.	amu	knit
pres. neg.	aman	knit not
pas. pos.	anda	did knit
pas. neg.	amananda	did not knit
fut. pos.	amoh	will knit
fut. neg.	amumai	will not knit
fut. pas. pos.	andaroh	will have knitted
fut. pas. neg.	amanandaroh	will not have knitted

CONDITIONAL

pres. pos.	ameba	if knits
pres. neg.	amaneba	if does not knit
pas. pos.	andara	if did knit
pas. neg.	amanandara	if did not knit
fut. pos.	amohnaraba	if would knit
fut. neg.	amumainaraba	if would not knit

IMPERATIVE

pos.	ame	do knit!
neg.	amuna	do not knit!

ADJECTIVAL

pos.	amu	knitting
neg.	amanu	not knitting

CONJUNCTIVE

pos.	ande	knit and
neg.	amanaide	knit not and

CONNECTIVE

pos.	ami-	....

SUBSTANTIVE

	ami	knitting

INTERROGATIVE

JAPANESE VERBS DEFINED IN ENGLISH
Continued from previous page (lower section)

forward.

Dohkeru (7 en) to play the buffoon; to jest.

Donaru (6 en) to roar with anger.

Donsuru (11b en) to become dull.

Dohsuru (11b en) what to do; how to act.

Egaku (3 ex) to draw, paint, portray, sketch, depict, describe.

Eguru (6 ex) to gouge, scoop out.

Enzuru (7a or 11b ex) to exercise, perform, play, act.

Erabu (1 ex) to select, choose, pick out, sort, assort.

Eramu (4 ex) same as **Erabu.**

Eru (7 ex) to get, obtain, have, gain possession; to be able to.

Continued on next page (lower section)

THE FOURTH CONJUGATION (b)

PART I. (all persons)		PART II. (1st and 3rd persons)	PART III. (2nd person)
INDICATIVE			
pres. pos.	amu	1. amimasu 2. oamiitasimasu 2. oamimohsimasu	1. oaminasaru 1. oamininaru 2. oaminasaimasu 2. oamininarimasu 2. oamiasobasu 3. oamiasobasimasu
pres. neg.	aman(ai)	1. amimasen 2. oamiitasimasen 2. oamimonsimasen	1. oaminasaran(ai) 1. oamininaran(ai) 2. oaminasaimasen 2. oamininarimasen 2. oamiasobasan(ai) 3. oamiasobasimasen
pas. pos.	anda	1. amimasita 2. oamiitasimasita 2. oamimohsimasita	1. oaminasatta 1. oamininatta 2. oaminasaimasita 2. oamininarimasita 2. oamiasobasita 3. oamiasobasimasita
pas. neg.	amananda amanakatta	1. amimasendesita 2. oamiitasimasendesita 2. oamimohsimasendesita	1. oaminasarananda 1. oaminasaranakatta 1. oamininarananda 1. oamininaranakatta 2. oaminasaimasendesita 2. oamininarimasendesita 2. oamiasobasananda 2. oamiasobasanakatta 3. oamiasobasimasendesita
fut. pos.	amoh	1. amimasyoh 2. oamiitasimasyoh 2. oamimohsimasyoh	1. oaminasaroh 1. oamininaroh 2. oaminasaimasyoh 2. oamininarimasyoh 3. oamiasobasimasyoh
fut. neg.	amumai	1. amimasumai 1. oamiitasimasumai 1. oamimohsimasumai	1. oaminasarumai 1. oamininarumai 2. oaminasaimasumai 2. oamininarimasumai 2. oamiasobasumai 3. oamiasobasimasumai
fut. pas. pos.	andaroh	1. amimasitaroh 2. oamiitasimasitaroh 2. oamimohsimasitaroh	1. oaminasattaroh 1. oamininattaroh 2. oaminasaimasitaroh 2. oamininarimasitaroh 2. oamiasobasitaroh 3. oamiasobasimasitaroh
		(-taroh or -tadesyoh, alternative)	
fut. pas. neg.	amanandaroh amanakattaroh	1. amimasendesitaroh 2. oamiitasimasendesitaroh 2. oamimohsimasendesitaroh	1. oaminasaranandaroh 1. oaminasaranakattaroh 1. oamininaranandaroh 1. oamininaranakattaroh 2. oaminasaimasendesitaroh 2. oamininarimasendesitaroh 2. oamiasobasanandaroh 2. oamiasobasanakattaroh 3. oamiasobasimasendesitaroh
		(-taroh or tadesyoh, -daroh or -dadesyoh, alternative)	

JAPANESE VERBS DEFINED IN ENGLISH
Continued from previous page (lower section)

(same as **Uru**).

Eru (6 ex) to select, Syn. of **Erabu.**

Essuru (11b en) to have an audience of; to be received in audience.

Gaisuru (11b ex) to harm, injure, hurt, damage, spoil.

Continued on next page (lower section)

24

Shinto Temple and Lantern

Noh Theater

CONDITIONAL

pres. pos.	ameba	1. amimasureba 2. oamiitasimasureba 2. oamimohsimasureba	1. oaminasareba 1. oamininareba 2. oaminasaimasureba 2. oamininarimasureba 2. oamiasobaseba 3. oamiasobasimasureba
pres. neg.	amaneba	1. amimasenkereba 2. oamiitasimaseneba 2. oamimohsimaseneba	1. oaminasaraneba 1. oamininaraneba 1. oamininarankereba 2. oaminasaimaseneba 2. oamininarimasenkereba 2. oamiasobasaneba 3. oamiasobasimasenkereba

(-seneba or -senkereba, alternative)

pas. pos.	andara(ba)	1. amimasitara(ba) 2. oamiitasimasitara(ba) 2. oamimohsimasitara(ba)	1. oaminasattara(ba) 1. oamininattara(ba) 2. oaminasaimasitara(ba) 2. oamininarimasitara(ba) 2. oamiasobasitara(ba) 3. oamiasobasimasitara(ba)
pas. neg.	amanandara(ba) amanakattara(ba) 1. amimasendesitara(ba) 2. oamiitasimasendesitara(ba) 2. oamimohsimasendesitara(ba)		1. oaminasaranandara(ba) 1. oaminasaranakattara(ba) 1. oamininaranandara(ba) 1. oamininaranakattara(ba) 2. oaminasaimasendesitara(ba) 2. oamininarimasendesitara(ba) 2. oamiasobasanandara(ba) 2. oamiasobasanakattara(ba) 3. oamiasobasimasendesitara(ba)
fut. pos.	amohnara(ba) 1. amimasyohnara(ba) 2. oamiitasimasyohnara(ba) 2. oamimohsimasyohnara(ba)		1. oaminasarohnara(ba) 1. oamininarohnara(ba) 2. oaminasaimasyohnara(ba) 2. oamininarimasyohnara(ba) 2. oamiasobasohnara(ba) 3. oamiasobasimasyohnara(ba)
fut. neg.	amumainara(ba) 1. amimasumainara(ba) 2. oamiitasimasumainara(ba) 2. oamimohsimasumainara(ba)		1. oaminasarumainara(ba) 1. oamininarumainara(ba) 2. oaminasaimasumainara(ba) 2. oamininarimasumainara(ba) 2. oamiasobasumainara(ba) 3. oamiasobasimasumainara(ba)

IMPERATIVE (addressed to 2d person only)

pos.	ame	1. oaminasai 2. oaminasaimase 2. oamiasobase 3. oamiasobasimase
neg.	amuna	1. oaminasaruna 2. oaminasaimasuna 2. oamiasobasuna 3. oamiasobasimasuna

---

JAPANESE VERBS DEFINED IN ENGLISH
Continued from previous page (lower section)

Ganbaru (6 en) to insist, persist.

-garu (6 suff.) to wish, to be willing; to be inclined; to long for. (-buru).

Gassuru (11b ex) to combine with; to unite with; to add, to sum up.

Gasuru (11b en) to celebrate; to congratulate; to lie down; to mount; to ride.

Gatatuku (3 en.) to jolt, bounce, shake.

Gebiru (7 en) to be vulgar; to be of low taste.

Gekisuru (11b en) to be excited; to be infuriated; to be enraged.

Genzuru (7a or 11b ex) to deduct, subtract, reduce, diminish.

Ginzuru (7a or 11b ex) to chant, recite.

Gisuru (11b ex) to imitate; to

Continued on next page (lower section)

ADJECTIVE

pos.   amu

1. amimasu(ru)	1. oaminasaru
2. oamiitasimasu(ru)	1. oamininaru
2. oamimohsimasu(ru)	2. oaminasaimasu(ru)
	2. oamininarimasu(ru)
	2. oamiasobasu
	3. oamiasobasimasu(ru)

neg.   aman(u)(ai)

1. amimasen(u)	1. oaminasaran(u)(ai)
2. oamiitasimasen(u)	1. oamininaran(u)(ai)
2. oamimohsimasen(u)	2. oaminasaimasen(u)
	2. oamininarimasen(u)
	2. oamiasobasan(u)(ai)
	3. oamiasobasimasen(u)

CONJUNCTIVE

pos.   ande

1. amimasite	1. oamininatte
2. oamiitasimasite	2. oaminasaimasite
2. oamimohsimasite	2. oamininarimasite
	2. oamiasobasite
	3. oamiasobasimasite

Also next to pos. line: 1. oaminasatte

neg.   amande
     amanaide
     amanakutte

1. amimasende(site)	1. oaminasaranaide
2. oamiitasimasende(site)	1. oamininaranaide
2. oamimohsimasende(site)	2. oaminasaimasende(site)
	2. oamininarimasende(site)
	2. oamiasobasanaide
	3. oamiasobasimasende(site)

(-naide or -nakutte, alternative)

CONNECTIVE ami-
SUBSTANTIVE ami

THE VERBS OF THE FOURTH CONJUGATION

About ten per cent of all Japanese verbs belong to this conjugation; the examples here are only a part of them.

Exo-active verbs	Endo-active verbs
Hasamu, to pinch	Isamu, to be gallant
Humu, to tread	Nayamu, to suffer
Kakomu, to surround	Sitasimu, to be intimate
Ogamu, to worship	Somu, to be stained
Osimu, to value	Sumu, to reside
Tanosimu, to enjoy	Tinamu, to be connected with
Tukamu, to grasp	Tizimu, to shrink
Tumu, to pluck	Tomu, to be rich
Uramu, to hate	Yamu, to fall sick
Yomu, to read	Yasumu, to repose

JAPANESE VERBS DEFINED IN ENGLISH
Continued from previous page (lower .section)

compare; to make believe.

 Gohsuru (11b ex) to name, title.

 Gomakasu (8 ex) to deceive, fake, bamboozle, cheat.

 Gorannasaru (6 ex) (ct. exp.) to see, look.

 Gosuru (11b en) to rank with;

to associate.

 Gozaru (6 en) to be, to exist.

 Gureru (7 en) to go astray; to go wrong; to get out of order.

 Guhsuru (11b ex) to treat; to wait on.

 Guzuru (6 ex) to importune for;

Continued on next page (lower section)

THE FIFTH CONJUGATION (a)

INDICATIVE

pres. pos.	sinu	die
pres. neg.	sinan	die not
pas. pos.	sinda	did die
pas. neg.	sinananda	did not die
fut. pos.	sinoh	will die
fut. neg.	sinumai	will not die
fut. pas. pos.	sindaroh	will have died
fut. pas. neg.	sinanandaroh	will not have died

CONDITIONAL

pres. pos.	sineba	if dies
pres. neg.	sinaneba	if does not die
pas. pos.	sindara	if did die
pas. neg.	sinanandara	if did not die
fut. pos.	sinohnaraba	if would die
fut. neg.	sinumainaraba	if would not die

IMPERATIVE

pos.	sine	die!
neg.	sinuna	do not die!

ADJECTIVAL

pos.	sinu	dying
neg.	sinanu	not dying

CONJUNCTIVE

pos.	sinde	die and
neg.	sinanaide	die not and

CONNECTIVE	sini-	....
SUBSTANTIVE	sini	death

INTERROGATIVE

JAPANESE VERBS DEFINED IN ENGLISH
Continued from previous page (lower section)

to tease with requests.

Gyosuru (11b ex) to ride, drive, control, manage, handle.

Gomenkohmuru (6 en) to be excused (ct. exp.)

Habakaru (6 ex) to dread; to be afraid of; to fear.

Habamu (4 ex) to oppose, obstruct, prevent, thwart.

Haberu (6 en) to attend to; to wait upon.

-haberu (ct. exp. suff.) to be. (obs.)

Habikoru (6 en) to overgrow, spread; to grow rampant.

Habuku (3 ex) to omit, leave out, dispense with.

Hadakaru (6 en) to be wide open.

Haeru (7 en) to grow; to look

Continued on page 29 (lower section)
27

THE FIFTH CONJUGATION (b)

	PART I. (all persons)	PART II. (1s and 3d persons)	PART III. (2d person)
INDICATIVE			
pres. pos.	sinu	1. sinimasu	1. osininasaru 2. osininasaimasu
pres. neg.	sinan(ai)	1. sinimasen	1. osininasaran(ai) 2. osininasaimasen
pas. pos.	sinda	1. sinimasita	1. osininasatta 2. osininasaimasita
pas. neg.	sinananda sinanakatta	1. sinimasendesita	1. osininasarananda 1. osininasaranakatta 2. osininasaimasendesita
fut. pos.	sinoh	1. sinimasyoh	1. osininasaroh 2. osininasaimasyoh
fut. neg.	sinumai	1. sinimasumai	1. osininasarumai 2. osininasaimasumai
fut. pas. pos.	sindaroh	1. sinimasitaroh	1. osininasattaroh 2. osininasaimasitaroh (-taroh or -tadesyoh, alternative)
fut. pas. neg.	sinanandaroh sinanakattaroh	1. sinimasendesitaroh	1. osininasaranandaroh 1. osininasaranakattaroh 2. osininasaimasendesitaroh (-daroh or -dadesyoh, alternative)
CONDITIONAL			
pres. pos.	sineba	1. sinimasureba	1. osininasareba 2. osininasaimasureba
pres. neg.	sinaneba	1. sinimasenkereba	1. osininasaraneba 2. osininasaimaseneba (-seneba or -senkereba, alternative)
pas. pos.	sindara(ba)	1. sinimasitara(ba)	1. osininasattara(ba) 2. osininasaimasitara(ba)
pas. neg.	sinanandara(ba) sinanakattara(ba)	1. sinimasendesitara(ba)	1. osininasaranandara(ba) 2. osininasaimasendesitara(ba)
fut. pos.	sinohnara(ba)	1. sinimasyohnara(ba)	1. osininasarohnara(ba) 2. osininasaimasyohnara(ba)
fut. neg.	sinumainara(ba)	1. sinimasumainara(ba)	1. osininasarumainara(ba) 2. osininasaimasumainara(ba)
IMPERATIVE (addressed to second person only)			
pos.	sine		1. osininasai 2. osininasaimase
neg.	sinuna		1. osininasaruna 2. osininasaimasuna
ADJECTIVE			
pos.	sinu(ru)	1. sinimasu(ru)	1. osininasaru 2. osininasaimasu(ru)
neg.	sinan(u)(ai)	1. sinimasen(u)	1. osininasaran(u)(ai) 2. osininasaimasen(u)
CONJUNCTIVE			
pos.	sinde	1. sinimasite	1. osininasatte 2. osininasaimasite
neg.	sinande sinanaide sinanakutte	1. sinimasende(site)	1. osininasaranaide 2. osininasaimasende(site) (-naide or -nakutte, alternative)
CONNECTIVE	sini-		
SUBSTANTIVE	sini		

There is no other verb than the one given in the fifth conjugation above. The verb SINU of this conjugation, being endo-active, does not allow a full conjugation as an exo-active verb. Besides, it belongs to the irregular verbs which may substitute other verbs at different degree of courteousness, for which see under the irregular conjugation.

THE SIXTH CONJUGATION (a)

INDICATIVE

pres. pos.	soru	shaves
pres. neg.	soran	does not shave
pas. pos.	sotta	did shave
pas. neg.	sorananda	did not shave
fut. pos.	soroh	will shave
fut. neg.	sorumai	will not shave
fut. pas. pos.	sottaroh	will have shaved
fut. pas. neg.	soranandaroh	will not have shaved

CONDITIONAL

pres. pos.	soreba	if shaves
pres. neg.	soraneba	if not shave
pas. pos.	sottara	if did shave
pas. neg.	soranandara	if did not shave
fut. pos.	sorohnaraba	if would shave
fut. neg.	sorumainaraba	if would not shave

IMPERATIVE

pos.	sore	shave!
neg.	soruna	do not shave!

ADJECTIVAL

pos.	soru	shaving
neg.	soranu	not shaving

CONJUNCTIVE

pos.	sotte	shave and
neg.	soranaide	shave not and

CONNECTIVE

	sori-	....

SUBSTANTIVE

	sori	shaving

INTERROGATIVE

JAPANESE VERBS DEFINED IN ENGLISH
Continued from page 27 (lower section)

well; to improve.

Hagasu (8 ex) to strip.

Hagemasu (8 ex) to encourage, urge.

Hagemu (4 en) to be industrious; to strive.

Hageru (7 en) to grow bald, to become bald; to come off; to peel.

Hagitoru (6 ex) to strip off; to rob; to deprive of.

Hagu (2 ex) to strip off, take off, join, pledge.

Hagukumu (4 ex) to bring up, rear, nourish.

Continued on next page (lower section)

THE SIXTH CONJUGATION (b)

INDICATIVE

	PART I (all persons)	PART II (1st & 3rd persons)	PART III (2d person)
pres. pos.	soru	1. sorimasu 2. osoriitasimasu 2. osorimohsimasu	1. osorinasaru 1. osorininaru 2. osorinasaimasu 2. osorininarimasu 2. osoriasobasu 3. osoriasobasimasu
pres. neg.	soran(ai)	1. sorimasen 2. osoriitasimasen 2. osorimohsimasen	1. osorinasaran(ai) 1. osorininaran(ai) 2. osorinasaimasen 2. osorininarimasen 2. osoriasobasan(ai) 3. osoriasobasimasen
pas. pos.	sotta	1. sorimasita 2. osoriitasimasita 2. osorimohsimasita	1. osorinasatta 1. osorininatta 2. osorinasaimasita 2. osorininarimasita 2. osoriasobasita 3. osoriasobasimasita
pas. neg.	sorananda soranakatta	1. sorimasendesita 2. osoriitasimasendesita 2. osorimohsimasendesita	1. osorinasarananda 1. osorinasaranakatta 1. osorininarananda 1. osorininaranakatta 2. osorinasaimasendesita 2. osorininarimasendesita 2. osoriasobasananda 2. osoriasobasanakatta 3. osoriasobasimasendesita
fut. pos.	soroh	1. sorimasyoh 2. osoriitasimasyoh 2. osorimohsimasyoh	1. osorinasaroh 1. osorininaroh 2. osorinasaimasyoh 2. osorininarimasyoh 3. osoriasobasimasyoh
fut. neg.	sorumai	1. sorimasumai 2. osoriitasimasumai 2. osorimohsimasumai	1. osorinasarumai 1. osorininarumai 2. osorinasaimasumai 2. osorininarimasumai 2. osoriasobasumai 3. osoriasobasimasumai
fut. pas. pos.	sottaroh	1. sorimasitaroh 2. osoriitasimasitaroh 2. osorimohsimasitaroh	1. osorinasattaroh 1. osorininattaroh 2. osorinasaimasitaroh 2. osorininarimasitaroh 2. osoriasobasitaroh 3. osoriasobasimasitaroh (-taroh or -tadesyoh, alternative)
fut. pas. neg.	soranandaroh	1. sorimasendesitaroh 2. osoriitasimasendesitaroh 2. osorimohsimasendesitaroh	1. osorinasaranandaroh 1. osorininaranandaroh 1. osorinasaranakattaroh 1. osorininaranakattaroh 2. osorinasaimasendesitaroh 2. osorininarimasendesitaroh 2. osoriasobasanandaroh 2. osoriasobasanakattaroh 3. osoriasobasimasendesitaroh (-daroh or -dadesyoh, alternative)

JAPANESE VERBS DEFINED IN ENGLISH
Continued from previous page (lower section)

Hagurakasu (8 ex) to let stray.

Hagurasu (8 ex) same as Hagurakasu.

Hagureru (7 en) to go astray, miss.

Haguru (6 ex) to turn up, uncover.

Hairu (6 en) to crawl into.

Continued on next page (lower section)

CONDITIONAL

pres. pos.	soreba	1. sorimasureba	1. osorinasareba

CONDITIONAL

pres. pos. soreba
1. sorimasureba
2. osoriitasimasureba
2. osorimohsimasureba

1. osorinasareba
1. osorininareba
2. osorinasaimasureba
2. osorininarimasureba
2. osoriasobaseba
3. osoriasobasimasureba

pres. neg. soraneba
1. sorimasenkereba
2. osoriitasimaseneba
2. osorimohsimaseneba

1. osorinasaraneba
1. osorininaraneba
1. osorinasarankereba
2. osorinasaimaseneba
2. osorininarimasenkereba
2. osoriasobasaneba
3. osoriasobasimasenkereba
(-seneba or -senkereba, alternative)

pas. pos. sottara (ba)
1. sorimasitara (ba)
2. osoriitasimasitara (ba)
2. osorimohsimasitara (ba)

1. osorinasattara (ba)
1. osorininattara (ba)
2. osorinasaimasitara (ba)
2. osorininarimasitara (ba)
2. osoriasobasitara (ba)
3. osoriasobasimasitara (ba)

pas. neg. soranandara (ba)
soranakattara (ba)
1. sorimasendesitara (ba)
2. osorimohsimasendesitara (ba)
2. osoriitasimasendesitara (ba)

1. osorinasaranandara (ba)
1. osorinasaranakattara (ba)
1. osorininaranandara (ba)
1. osorininaranakattara (ba)
2. osorinasaimasendesitara (ba)
2. osorininarimasendesitara (ba)
2. osoriasobasanandara (ba)
2. osoriasobasanakattara (ba)
3. osoriasobasimasendesitara (ba)

fut. pos. sorohnaraba
1. sorimasyohnara (ba)
2. osoriitasimasyohnara (ba)
2. osorimohsimasyohnara (ba)

1. osorinasarohnara (ba)
1. osorininarohnara (ba)
2. osorinasaimasyohnara (ba)
2. osorininarimasyohnara (ba)
2. osoriasobasohnara (ba)
3. osoriasobasimasyohnara (ba)

fut. neg. sorumainaraba
1. sorimasumainara (ba)
2. osoriitasimasumainara (ba)
2. osorimohsimasumainara (ba)

1. osorinasarumainara (ba)
1. osorininarumainara (ba)
2. osorinasaimasumainara (ba)
2. osorininarimasumainara (ba)
2. osoriasobasumainara (ba)
3. osoriasobasimasumainara (ba)

IMPERATIVE (addressed to second person only)

pos. sore

1. osorinasai
2. osorinasaimase
2. osoriasobase
3. osoriasobasimase

neg. soruna

1. osorinasaruna
2. osorinasaimasuna
2. osoriasobasuna
3. osoriasobasimasuna

JAPANESE VERBS DEFINED IN ENGLISH
Continued from previous page (lower section)

Haimawaru (6 en) to crawl about.

Hairu (6 en) to enter, penetrate, contain, join, admit.

Haisuru (11b ex) to worship, receive; to be appointed, to venerate; marry, mate, pair, expel, dethrone, abolish.

Hakadoru (6 en) to make progress.

Hakarau (10 ex) to manage, arrange.

Hakaru (6 ex) to calculate, estimate, weigh, measure, sound, survey, consult, confer with.

Hakeru (7 en) to flow, run out; to be in demand.

Hakitigaeru (7 ex) to wear the wrong shoe; to misunderstand.

Hakidasu (8 ex) to vomit, spit

Continued on next page (lower section)

ADJECTIVE

pos.	soru	1. sorimasu(ru)	1. osorinasaru
		2. osoriitasimasu(ru)	1. osorininaru
		2. osorimohsimasu(ru)	2. osorinasaimasu(ru)
			2. osorininarimasu(ru)
			2. osoriasobasu
			3. osoriasobasimasu(ru)
neg.	soranu	1. sorimasen(u)	1. osorinasaran(u)(ai)
		2. osoriitasimasen(u)	1. osorininaran(u)(ai)
		2. osorimohsimasen(u)	2. osorinasaimasen(u)
			2. osorininarimasen(u)
			2. osoriasobasan(u)(ai)
			3. osoriasobasimasen(u)

CONJUNCTIVE

pos.	sotte	1. sorimasite	1. osorinasatte
		2. osoriitasimasite	1. osorininatte
		2. osorimohsimasite	2. osorinasaimasite
			2. osorininarimasite
			2. osoriasobasite
			3. osoriasobasimasite
neg.	soranaide	1. sorimasende(site)	1. osorinasaranaide
		2. osoriitasimasende(site)	1. osorininaranaide
		2. osorimohsimasende(site)	2. osorinasaimasende(site)
			2. osorininarimasende(site)
			2. osoriasobasanaide
			3. osoriasobasimasende(site)

(-naide or -nakutta, alternative)

CONNECTIVE
sori-

SUBSTANTIVE
sori

THE VERBS OF THE SIXTH CONJUGATION

About 25 per cent of all Japanese verbs belong to this conjugation. The few examples are given here.

Exo-active verbs	Endo-active verbs
Hakaru, to measure	**Ataru,** to touch
Horu, to dig	**Hasiru,** to run
Keru, to kick	**Hikaru,** to shine
Kiru, to cut	**Kakeru,** to gallop
Kukuru, to tie	**Kumoru,** to be cloudy
Mamoru, to defend	**Minoru,** to bear fruit
Maturu, to celebrate	**Nemuru,** to sleep
Musiru, to pluck	**Noru,** to get on
Saegiru, to cross	**Saeduru,** to sing
Seru, to auction	**Suberu,** to slip
Yaru, to let go	**Tiru,** to be scattered
Yuduru, to give	**Yoru,** to depend on

JAPANESE VERBS DEFINED IN ENGLISH

Continued from previous page (lower section)

out; emit, sweep out.

Hakikaeru (7 ex) to change one's shoes, clogs, etc.

Hakiyoseru (7 ex) to sweep into a heap.

Hakobu (1 ex) to carry, transport.

Hakobu (1 en) to progress, advance.

Haku (3 ex) to vomit, spit,

Continued on next page (lower section)

Imperial Palace

Kiyomizu Temple, Kyoto

THE SEVENTH CONJUGATION (a)

INDICATIVE

pres. pos.	ageru	raises
pres. neg.	agen	raises not
pas. pos.	ageta	did raise
pas. neg.	agenanda	did not raise
fut. pos.	ageyoh	will raise
fut. neg.	agemai	will not raise
fut. pas. pos.	agetaroh	will have raised
fut.pas.neg.	agenandaroh	will not have raised

CONDITIONAL

pres. pos.	agereba	if raises
pres. neg.	ageneba	if does not raise
pas. pos.	agetara	if did raise
pas. neg.	agenandara	if did not raise
fut. pos.	ageyohnaraba	if would raise
fut. neg.	agemainaraba	if would not raise

IMPERATIVE

pos.	ageyo	raise!
neg.	agena	do not raise!

ADJECTIVAL

pos.	ageru	raising
neg.	agenu	not raising

CONJUNCTIVE

pos.	agete	raises and
neg.	agenaide	raises not and

CONNECTIVE

	age-	....

SUBSTANTIVE

	age	raise

INTERROGATIVE

JAPANESE VERBS DEFINED IN ENGLISH
Continued from previous page (lower section)

emit, wear, drain off, sweep.

Hakusuru (11b ex) to gain, win.

Hamaru (6 en) to fit; to fall into, plunge; to be addicted with.

Hamekomu (4 ex) to inlay in; insert in, plunge into, ensnare.

Hameru (7 ex) to fit in, set in, inlay, mount, apply to, put in.

Hamidasu (8 en) to protrude, bulge out.

Hamideru (7 en) same as **Hami-**dasu.

Hamu (4 ex) to eat, feed on.

Hanareru (7 en) to separate from, part, get loose, escape.

Hanasaku (3 en) to bloom.

Hanasikakeru (7 en) to accost, address.

Hanasu (8 en) to say, speak.

Hanasu (8 ex) to detach, disjoin, isolate.

Hanatu (9 ex) to let go, release,

Continued on next page (lower section)

THE SEVENTH CONJUGATION (b)

INDICATIVE	PART I (all persons)	PART II (1st and 3d persons)	PART III (2d person)
pres. pos.	ageru	1. agemasu 2. oageitasimasu 3. oagemohsimasu	1. oagenasaru 1. oageninaru 2. oagenasaimasu 2. oageninarimasu 2. oageasobasu 3. oageasobasimasu
pres. neg.	agen(ai)	1. agemasen 2. oageitasimasen 2. oagemohsimasen	1. oagenasaran(ai) 1. oageninaran(ai) 2. oagenasaimasen 2. oageninarimasen 2. oageasobasan(ai) 3. oageasobasimasen
pas. pos.	ageta	1. agemasita 2. oageitasimasita 2. oagemohsimasita	1. oagenasatta 1. oageninatta 2. oagenasaimasita 2. oageninarimasita 2. oageasobasita 3. oageasobasimasita
pas. neg.	agenanda agenakatta	1. agemasendesita 2. oageitasimasendesita 2. oagemohsimasendesita	1. oagenasarananda 1. oagenasaranakatta 1. oageninarananda 1. oageninaranakatta 2. oagenasaimasendesita 2. oageninarimasendesita 2. oageasobasananda 2. oageasobasanakatta 3. oageasobasimsendesita
fut. pos.	ageyoh	1. agemasyoh 2. oageitasimasyoh 2. oagemohsimasyoh	1. oagenasaroh 1. oageninaroh 2. oagenasaimasyoh 2. oageninarimasyoh 3. oageasobasimasyoh
fut. neg.	agemai	1. agemasumai 2. oageitasimasumai 2. oagemohsimasumai	1. oagenasarumai 1. oageninarumai 2. oagenasaimasumai 2. oageninarimasumai 2. oageasobasumai 3. oageasobasimasumai
fut. pas. pos.	agetaroh	1. agemasitaroh 2. oageitasimasitaroh 2. oagemohsimasitaroh	1. oagenasattaroh 1. oageninattaroh 2. oagenasaimasitaroh 2. oageninarimasitaroh 2. oageasobasitaroh 3. oageasobasimasitaroh (-taroh or tadesyoh, alternative)
fut. pas. neg.	agenandaroh agenakattaroh	1. agemasendesitaroh 2. oageitasimasendesitaroh 2. oagemohsimasendesitaroh	1. oagenasaranandaroh 1. oageninaranandaroh 1. oagenasaranakattaroh 1. oageninaranakattaroh 2. oagenasaimasendesitaroh 2. oageninarimasendesitaroh 2. oageasobasanandaroh 2. oageasobasanakattaroh 3. oageasobasimasendesitaroh (-daroh or -dadesyoh, alternative)

JAPANESE VERBS DEFINED IN ENGLISH
Continued from previous page (lower section)

let fly, fire, emit. | tend.

Hanberu (6 en) to wait on, at- | **Hanekaesu** (8 ex) to bounce.

Continued on next page (lower section)

pres. pos.	agereba	1. agemasureba	1. oagenasareba
		2. oageitasimasureba	1. oageninareba
		2. oagemohsimasureba	2. oagenasaimasureba
			2. oageninarimasureba
			2. oageasobaseba
			3. oageasobasimasureba

pres. neg.	ageneba	1. agemasenkereba	1. oagenasaraneba
		2. oageitasimaseneba	1. oageninaraneba
		2. oagemohsimaseneba	1. oagenasarankereba
			2. oagenasaimaseneba
			2. oageninarimasenkereba
			2. oageasobasaneba
			3. oageasobasimasenkereba

(-seneba or -senkereba, alternative)

pas. pos.	agetara		1. oagenasattara (ba)
		1. agemasitara (ba)	1. oageninattara (ba)
		2. oageitasimasitara (ba)	2. oagenasaimasitara (ba)
		2. oagemohsimasitara (ba)	2. oageninarimasitara (ba)
			2. oageasobasitara (ba)
			3. oageasobasimasitara (ba)

pas. neg.	agenandara		1. oagenasaranandara (ba)
		1. agemasendesitara (ba)	1. oagenasaranakattara (ba)
		2. oageitasimasendesitara (ba)	1. oageninaranandara (ba)
		2. oagemohsimasendesitara (ba)	1. oageninaranakattara (ba)
			2. oagenasaimasendesitara (ba)
			2. oageninarimasendesitara (ba)
			2. oageasobasanandara (ba)
			2. oageasobasanakattara (ba)
			3. oageasobasimasendesitara (ba)

fut. pos.	ageyohnaraba		1. oagenasarohnara (ba)
		1. agemasyohnara (ba)	1. oageninarohnara (ba)
		2. oageitasimasyohnara (ba)	2. oagenasaimasyohnara (ba)
		2. oagemohsimasyohnara (ba)	2. oageninarimasyohnara (ba)
			2. oageasobasohnara (ba)
			3. oageasobasimasyohnara (ba)

fut. neg.	agemainara (ba)		1. oagenasarumainara (ba)
		1. agemasumainara (ba)	1. oageninarumainara (ba)
		2. oageitasimasumainara (ba)	2. oageninarimasumainara (ba)
		2. oagemohsimasumainara (ba)	2. oagenasaimasumainara (ba)
			2. oageasobasumainara (ba)
			3. oageasobasimasumainara (ba)

JAPANESE VERBS DEFINED IN ENGLISH

Continued from previous page (lower section)

Hanemawaru (6 en) to bounce about.

Haneokiru (7 en) to jump up.

Haneru (7 en) to leap, jump, romp, spatter, rebound, behead, reject.

Hanziru (7a ex) to decipher, interpret, divine, judge.

Hansuru (11b en) to oppose, go against, rebel.

Haramu (4 en) to conceive, become pregnant.

Harasu (8 ex) to clear up, dissipate, swell, inflate.

Harau (10 ex) to pay, sweep away.

Hareru (7 en) to become clear; to clear up; to swell up.

Hariageru (7 en) to raise, elevate.

Hariau (10 en) to compete with, strive with.

Harikiru (6 en) to extend to full; to strain.

Harikomu (4 en) to exert oneself.

Harisakeru (7 en) to burst open.

Haritaosu (8 ex) to knock down.

Haru (6 ex) to stretch, spread, paste.

Continued on next page (lower section)

IMPERATIVE (addressed to second person only)

neg. agena

1. oagenasai
2. oagenasaimase
2. oageasobase
3. oageasobasimase

pos. ageyo

1. oagenasaruna
2. oagenasaimasuna
2. oageasobasuna
3. oageasobasimasuna

ADJECTIVE

pos. ageru

1. agemasu(ru)
2. oageitasimasu(ru)
2. oagemohsimasu(ru)

1. oagenasaru
1. oageninaru
2. oagenasaimasu(ru)
2. oageninarimasu(ru)
2. oageasobasu
3. oageasobasimasu(ru)

neg. agenu

1. agemasen(u)
2. oageitasimasen(u)
2. oagemohsimasen(u)

1. oagenasaran(u)(ai)
1. oageninaran(u)(ai)
2. oagenasaimasen(u)
2. oageninarimasen(u)
2. oageasobasan(u)(ai)
3. oageasobasimasen(u)

CONJUNCTIVE

pos. agete

1. agemasite
2. oageitasimasite
2. oagemohsimasite

1. oagenasatte
1. oageninatte
2. oagenasaimasite
2. oageninarimasite
2. oageasobasite
3. oageasobasimasite

neg. agenaide

1. agemasende(site)
2. oageitasimasende(site)
2. oagemohsimasende(site)

1. oagenasaranaide
1. oageninaranaide
2. oagenasaimasende(site)
2. oageninarimasende(site)
2. oageasobasanaide
3. oageasobasimasende(site)

(-naide or nakutte, alternative)

CONNECTIVE
age-
SUBSTANTIVE
age

JAPANESE VERBS DEFINED IN ENGLISH
Continued from previous page (lower section)

Harumeku (3 en) to look like spring.

Hasamaru (6 en) to lie between.

Hasamu (4 ex) to pinch; to hold between; to shear, cut.

Haseru (7 ex) to drive.

Haseru (7 en) to run.

Hasirasu (8 ex) to run, sail; to put to run.

Hasiru (6 en) to run, sail.

Hassuru (11b ex) to start, leave, depart.

Hasuru (11b ex) to send out, dispatch.

Hataku (3 ex) to beat, strike, dust.

Hatarakasu (8 ex) to set to work, employ.

Hataraku (3 en) to work.

Hatasu (8 ex) to accomplish, carry out, perform, fulfill.

Hateru (7 en) to end, terminate, die.

Hau (10 en) to crawl, creep.

Hayamaru (6 en) to be rash.

Hayameru (7 ex) to quicken, hasten.

Hayaru (6 en) to prevail; to be in fashion; to be impatient.

Hayasu (8 ex) to applaud, play music; to cut into slices; to let grow.

Hazeru (7 en) to burst open; to crinkle.

Haziiru (6 en) to be ashamed of.

Hazikakasu (8 ex) to put to

Continued on next page (lower section)

THE VERBS OF THE SEVENTH CONJUGATION

By far the greater portion of Japanese verbs belong to this conjugation. About 30 per cent of simple verbs and all of derived verbs come under this class.

The examples of the simple verbs:

Exo-active verbs	Endo-active verbs
abiru, to pour over	areru, to be stormy
ateru, to touch	hareru, to clear up
homeru, to praise	haziru, to be ashamed
kiseru, to dress	hoeru, to howl
miru, to see	ikiru, to live
niru, to boil	kogeru, to be scorched
sageru, to lower	nagaraeru, to live long
toziru, to close	neru, to sleep
ueru, to plant	otiru, to fall
ukeru, to receive	otoroeru, to weaken
wasureru, to forget	sugiru, to exceed

THE DERIVATIVE VERBS

When verbs as, **sareru** (to be acted upon), **eru** (to be able to), **saseru** (to let do) etc. in modified form, are attached to a simple verb, they make new verbs with meaning modified from the original. These latter are called the derivative verbs.

For example: From the simple verb **kiku** (to hear), following verbs are derived:

passive	kikareru,	to be heard by.
potential	kikeru, kikareru, kikoeru,	can be heard; to be capable of hearing; to be worthy of hearing.
compulsive-active	kikasu, kikaseru,	to let hear.
compulsive-passive	kikasareru,	to be made to hear.
compulsive-potential	kikasareru,	to be able to let hear.

JAPANESE VERBS DEFINED IN ENGLISH
Continued from previous page (lower section)

shame.

Hazikaku (3 en) to be put to shame.

Hazikeru (7 en) to split open, pop.

Haziku (3 en) to spring, flip, refuse, repel, exclude.

Hazimaru (6 en) to begin, com-mence.

Hazimeru (7 ex) to begin to commence.

Haziru (7 en) to be ashamed.

Hazisimeru (7 ex) to put to shame.

Hazukasigeru (6 en) to be shy, bashful, ashamed.

Continued on next page (lower section)

All the derivative verbs end in -eru and belong to the seventh conjugation, except in one instance, where it ends in -su and belongs to the eighth conjugation.

The derivative verbs from verbs of all conjugations are given in the list herewith:

active (endo or exo)	passive	potential	compulsive active	compulsive passive	compulsive potential
1 erabu	erabareru	eraberu	erabasu erabaseru	erabasareru	erabasareru
2 aogu	aogareru	aogeru	aogasu aogaseru	aogasareru	aogasareru
3 kaku	kakareru	kakeru	kakasu kakaseru	kakasareru	kakasareru
4 amu	amareru	ameru	amasu amaseru	amasareru	amasareru
5 sinu	sinareru	sineru	sinasu sinaseru	sinasareru	sinasareru
6 soru	sorareru	soreru	sorasu soraseru	sorasareru	sorasareru
7 ageru	agerareru	agerareru	agesasu agesaseru	agesaserareru	agesaserareru
7a uru eru	erareru	erareru	esasu esaseru	esaserareru	esaserareru
7a -zuru -ziru	-zirareru	-zirareru	-zisasu -zisaseru	-zisaserareru	-zisaserareru
8 hosu	hosareru	hoseru	hosasu hosaseru	hosaserareru	hosaserareru
9 matu	matareru	materu	matasu mataseru	matasareru	matasareru
10 arau	arawareru	araeru	arawasu arawaseru	arawasareru	arawasareru
11a kuru	korareru	korareru	kosasu kosaseru	kosaserareru	kosaserareru
11b suru	serareru sareru	serareru	sasu saseru	saserareru	saserareru
11c inuru	inareru	ineru	inasu inaseru	inasareru	inasareru

JAPANESE VERBS DEFINED IN ENGLISH
Continued from previous page (lower section)

Hazukasimeru (7 ex) to insult, humiliate, violate.

Hazumu (4 en) to spring, bound; to rise in spirit.

Hazureru (7 en) to deviate from, come off; to be disjointed; to go wrong.

Hazusu (8 ex) to unfasten, disconnect.

Hedataru (6 en) to be partition-

Continued on next page (lower section)

In the foregoing table, it is seen that the passive is formed from the root verb and -sareru; for example: **matu** (to wait) and **-sareru** (to be acted upon) are contracted into **matareru** (to be waited): the potential is formed from the root verb and -eru, thus: **amu** (to knit) and **-eru** (to be able to) are contracted into **ameru** (to be able to knit): the compulsive-active is formed from the root verb and **-saru** or **-saseru**, thus; **soru** (to shave) and **-sasu** or **saseru** (to let do) are contracted into **sorasu, soraseru** (to let shave): the compulsive passive is formed from the root verb and **-sasareru** or **saserareru**, thus; **arau** (to ash) and **-sasareru** or **saserareru** (to be made to do) are contracted into **arawasareru** (to be made to wash): the compulsive potential is formed from the root verb and **-sasare-eru** or **saserare-eru**, thus; **kaku** (to write) and **-sasare-eru** or **saserare-eru** (to be capable of being made to do) are contracted into **kakasareru** (to be capable of being made to write). The compulsive passive and compulsion potential are always alike in form.

In some special speech, certain verbs in passive or compulsive form are used in extremely courteous expression. In these cases, though in passive form, the verbs have active sense.

Another sort of derivative verbs may be formed from many endo-active verbs changing into exo-active verbs in a peculiar manner, nearly simulating the compulsive-active. The conjugation is also changed from 2nd, 3rd, 4th, 6th, or 7th into 3rd, 6th, 7th, or 8th. In these cases the endo- or exo-active verbs are either of 7th or 8th conjugation.

The change from the endo-active verb into exo-active verb is effected by

1. The change of the stem vowel from A to E, and the change of the conjugation from 6th to 7th. The examples:

agaru, to go up.	ageru, to raise.
ataru, to touch.	ateru, to let touch.
azukaru, to take in custody.	azukeru, to put in trust.
hamaru,to plunge.	hameru, to put in.
husaru, to stoop down.	huseru, to put face down.
kakaru, to hang.	kakeru, to hang.

JAPANESE VERBS DEFINED IN ENGLISH
Continued from previous page (lower section)

ed; distant; to become far.

Hedateru (7 ex) to part, separate, prevent.

Heisuru (11b ex) to engage to a position.

Hekomasu (8 ex) to depress, dent, humiliate, crush.

Hekomu (4 en) to be indented; to collapse, yield.

Hensuru (11b en) to lean toward, incline to.

Hensuru (11b ex) to reduce to, belittle.

Henzuru (7 or 11b en) to change to.

Henzuru (7a or 11b ex) to change, alter.

Herikudaru (6 en) to humble oneself.

Heru (6 en) to decrease, fall, sin; to pass, elapse, warp.

Heturau (10 en) to flatter.

Hiagaru (6 en) to dry up.

Hibiku (3 en) to resound, echo; to affect.

Hieru (7 en) to grow cold, chill,

Continued on next page (lower setion)

makaru, to be able to make cheaper	makeru, to cut price.
osamaru, to calm.	osameru, to pacify.
simaru, to be shut.	simeru, to shut.
somaru, to be dyed.	someru, to dye.
sutaru, to be lost.	suteru, to throw away.
tamaru, to accumulate.	tameru, to save.
tomaru, to stand still.	tomeru, to check movement.
tukaru, to be steeped.	tukeru, to steep.
tumaru, to be plugged up.	tumeru, to plug up.
tutomaru, to be able to work.	tutomeru, to work.
umaru, to be filled up.	umeru, to fill up.
wakaru, to be divided.	wakeru, to divide.
yudaru, to be boiled.	yuderu, to boil.
kawaru, to change.	kaeru, to exchange.
mazaru, to get mixed up.	mazeru, to mix up.
maziwaru, to intercourse.	mazieru, to let come together.
magaru, to be bent.	mageru, to bend.
kiwamaru, to come to limit.	kiwameru, to go to limit.
sadamaru, to become fixed.	sadameru, to fix.

2. The change of r into s in the ending, and the change of conjugation from 7th to 8th. The examples:

iburu, to smoke.	ibusu, to smoke.
kaeru, to go back.	kaesu, to give back.
kawaru, to remove.	kawasu, to change place.
mawaru, to go round.	mawasu, to spin.
naoru, to heal.	naosu, to cure.
naru, to become.	nasu, to do.
nigoru, to become cloudy.	nigosu, to make cloudy.
nokoru, to remain.	nokosu, to let remain.
uturu, to move.	utusu, to let move.

3. The change of the ending from that of 7th into that of the 8th conjugation, together with change in stem vowel. Examples:

deru, to go out.	dasu, to let out.
hueru, to increase.	huyasu, to increase.
hukeru, to grow late.	hukasu, to delay at night.
ieru, to heal.	iyasu, to cure.
ikiru, to live.	ikasu, to let live.
kareru, to wither.	karasu, to let wither.
koeru, to grow fat.	koyasu, to make fat.
makeru, to lose.	makasu, to defeat.
nareru, to get used to.	narasu, to make get used to.
tukareru, to get tired.	tukarasu, to make tired.

JAPANESE VERBS DEFINED IN ENGLISH
Continued from previous page (lower section)

cool.

Higamu (4 en) to be suspicious; to be warped.

Hiideru (7 en) to surpass, excell.

Hikaeru (7 en) to hold back, restrain.

Hikarabiru (7 en) to dry up, parch, shrivel.

Hikarasu (8 ex) to make glitter, shine, brighten, polish.

Hikaru (6 en) to shine, blaze, glimmer, sparkle, flash.

Continued on next page (lower section)

Kabuki Theater

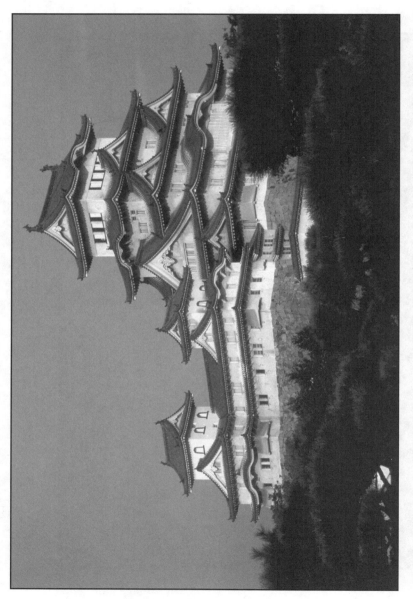

Himeji Castle

4. The change of the final vowel of the 4th conjugation into the ending of the 7th conjugation. The examples:

yamu, to cease.
yasumu, to take a rest.
yurumu, to become loose.

yameru, to stop.
yasumeru, to rest.
yurumeru, to make loose.

5. The change of the ending of the 7th conjugation eru into u, at the same time changing the conjugation to that of the 6th. The examples:

kureru, to become hollow.
tureru, to be fished up.
wareru, to be broken.
yureru, to be shaken.

kuru, to dig hollow.
turu, to fish.
waru, to break.
yuru, to shake.

6. The change of the ending from that of the 7th into that of the 8th conjugation, with the reduction of a syllable. The examples:

konareru, to get digested.
nagareru, to flow.
yogoreru, to be soiled.

konasu, to digest.
nagasu, to let flow.
yogosu, to soil.

7. The change of the ending of the 7th conjugation into u, at the same time changing the conjugation into that of the 3rd. Examples:

kuzikeru, to be demolished.
tokeru, to dissolve, to loosen.
yakeru, to get burned.

kuziku, to demolish.
toku, to dissolve, to untie.
yaku, to burn.

8. The change of the final vowel u of the 3rd conjugation into the ending of the 7th conjugation. Examples:

aku, to become open.
tuku, to adhere.

akeru, to open.
tukeru, to attach.

JAPANESE VERBS DEFINED IN ENGLISH
Continued from previous page (lower section)

Hikasareru (7 en) to be drawn, dragged.

Hikaseru (7 ex) to cause to withdraw.

Hikatamaru (6 en) to dry up and harden.

Hikeru (7 en) to lose courage; to break up.

Hikiageru (7 ex) to raise, hoist; to promote, withdraw.

Hikiakeru (7 ex) to pull open.

Hikiau (10 en) to pay; to be profitable; to pull in opposite direction.

Hikiawasu (8 ex) to compare, check; to bring together, introduce.

Hikidasu (8 ex) to draw out, drag out.

Hikihagasu (8 ex) to strip off, tear off, uncover.

Hikihagu (2 ex) to strip off, tear off, uncover.

Hikihanasu (8 ex) to pull apart, tear apart.

Hikiharau (10 en) to evacuate, vacate.

Hikihazusu (8 ex) to pull out of place, take down.

Hikiiru (7 ex) to lead, head.

Hikikaeru (7 ex) to exchange, convert.

Hikikiru (6 ex) to pull apart.

Hikikomoru (6 en) to keep in-

Continued on next page (lower section)

9. The change of the final vowel **u** of the 10th conjugation into **wasu** of the 8th conjugation. Examples:

kuu, to eat.	kuwasu, to let eat.
wadurau, to suffer.	wadurawasu, to make suffer.

10. The change of conjugation from 6th to 7th with an increase of a syllable. The example:

iru, to go in.	ireru, to put in.

11. The change of the final vowel **u** of the 2nd conjugation into the ending of the 7th conjugation. The example:

kasigu, to lean.	kasigeru, to incline.

12. The change in stem vowel only, both in 7th conjugation. Example:

nieru, to boil up.	niru, to boil.

7a CONJUGATION

This is an irregular conjugation belonging to the 7th conjugation The irregularity is limited to the indicative present positive. They are:

> uru or)
> eru   )   to get.
>
> -zuru or)
> -ziru   )   to do (a suffix verb analogous to -suru).*

In these verbs, only the first of the alternatives, i. e. **uru** and **-zuru** are irregular. The regular conjugation is made from **eru** and **-ziru** in the manner as given under the 7th conjugation.

* This suffix is used with some of the nominal verbs consisting of a single Chinese character with Chinese sound, which are usually suffixed with -suru of 11-b conjugation. See under that conjugation. Sometimes -zuru, -ziru are also conjugated as -suru.

JAPANESE VERBS DEFINED IN ENGLISH
Continued from previous page (lower section)

doors; to be confined to one's bed.

Hikikomu (4 ex) to take, catch.

Hikikomu (4 en) to go in, retreat.

Hikikorosu (8 ex) to kill by running over.

Hikikuraberu (7 ex) to compare with.

Hikikurumeru (7 ex) to bring together; to make into a bundle; to include, summarize, generalize.

Hikimatomeru (7 ex) to bring together.

Hikimodosu (8 ex) to bring back, restore.

Hikimuku (3 ex) to peel, pull off, strip off.

Hikimusiru (6 ex) to pull off, tear off, pluck.

Hikinaosu (8 ex) to return to, recover, restore.

Hikinobasu (8 ex) to draw out, stretch, extend, enlarge.

Hikinuku (3 ex) to pull out, pluck, extract, pick out, select.

Hikiokosu (8 ex) to raise up, lead to, provoke; to revive.

Hikiorosu (8 ex) to drag down.

Hikisagaru (6 en) to retire, withdraw, leave.

Hikisageru (7 ex) to lower, bring down, reduce, degrade.

Continued on next page (lower section)

THE EIGHTH CONJUGATION (a)

INDICATIVE

pres. pos.	osu	presses
pres. neg.	osan	does not press
pas. pos.	osita	did press
pas. neg.	osananda	did not press
fut. pos.	osoh	will press
fut. neg.	osumai	will not press
fut. pas. pos.	ositaroh	will have pressed
fut. pas. neg.	osanandaroh	will not have pressed

CONDITIONAL

pres. pos.	oseba	if presses
pres. neg.	osaneba	if does not press
pas. pos.	ositara	if did press
pas. neg.	osanandara	if did not press
fut. pos.	osohnaraba	it would press
fut. neg.	osumainaraba	if would not press

IMPERATIVE

pos.	ose	do press!
neg.	osuna	do not press!

ADJECTIVAL

pos.	osu	pressing
neg.	osanu	not pressing

CONJUNCTIVE

pos.	osite	presses and
neg.	osanaide	presses not and

CONNECTIVE

	osi-	....

SUBSTANTIVE

	osi	pressure

INTERROGATIVE

JAPANESE VERBS DEFINED IN ENGLISH
Continued from previous page (lower section)

Hikisaru (6 ex) to deduct, subtract.

Hikisimaru (6 en) to become tense; to tighten.

Hikisimeru (7 en) to strain, tighten, make firm.

Hikitateru (7 ex) to patronize, favor; to recommend, encourage; to keep up; to drag off.

Hikitatu (9 en) to look well; to become active.

Hikitigiru (6 ex) to pull off, tear

Continued on next page (lower section)

THE EIGHTH CONJUGATION (b)

	PART I (all persons)	PART II (1st & 3rd persons)	PART III (2nd person)
INDICATIVE			
pres. pos.	osu	1. osimasu 2. oosiitasimasu 2. oosimohsimasu	1. oosinasaru 1. oosininaru 2. oosinasaimasu 2. oosininarimasu 2. oosiasobasu 3. oosiasobasimasu
pres. neg.	osan(ai)	1. osimasen 2. oosiitasimasen 2. oosimohsimasen	1. oosinasaran(ai) 1. oosininaran(ai) 2. oosinasaimasen 2. oosininarimasen 2. oosiasobasan(ai) 3. oosiasobasimasen
pas. pos.	osita	1. osimasita 2. oosiitasimasita 2. oosimohsimasita	1. oosinasatta 1. oosininatta 2. oosinasaimasita 2. oosininarimasita 2. oosiasobasita 3. oosiasobasimasita
pas. neg.	osananda osanakatta	1. osimasendesita 2. oosiitasimasendesita 2. oosimohsimasendesita	1. oosinasarananda 1. oosinasaranakatta 1. oosininarananda 1. oosininaranakatta 2. oosinasaimasendesita 2. oosininarimasendesita 2. oosiasobasananda 2. oosiasobasanakatta 3. oosiasobasimasendesita
fut. pos.	osoh	1. osimasyoh 2. oosiitasimasyoh 2. oosimohsimasyoh	1. oosinasaroh 1. oosininaroh 2. oosinasaimasyoh 2. oosininarimasyoh 3. oosiasobasimasyoh
fut. neg.	osumai	1. osimasumai 2. oosiitasimasumai 2. oosimohsimasumai	1. oosinasarumai 1. oosininarumai 2. oosinasaimasumai 2. oosininarimasumai 2. oosiasobasumai 3. oosiasobasimasumai
fut. pas. pos.	ositaroh	1. osimasitaroh 2. oosiitasimasitaroh 2. oosimohsimasitaroh	1. oosinasattaroh 1. oosininattaroh 2. oosinasaimasitaroh 2. oosininarimasitaroh 2. oosiasobasitaroh 3. oosiasobasimasitaroh

(-taroh or -tadesyoh, alternative)

| **fut. pas. neg.** | osanandaroh | 1. osimasendesitaroh
2. oosiitasimasendesitaroh
2. ooshimohsimasendesitaroh | 1. oosinasaranandaroh
1. oosininaranandaroh
1. oosinasaranakattaroh
1. oosininaranakattaroh
2. oosinasaimasendesitaroh
2. oosininarimasendesitaroh
2. oosiasobasanandaroh
2. oosiasobasanakattaroh
3. oosiasobasimasendesitaroh |

(-daroh or -dadesyoh, alternative)

JAPANESE VERBS DEFINED IN ENGLISH
Continued from previous page (lower section)

off.

Hikitomeru (7 ex) to detain; to check, keep back.

Hikitoru (6 ex) to take back; to receive.

Hikitoru (6 en) to withdraw, re-

Continued on next page (lower section)

pres. pos.	oseba	1. osimasureba	1. oosinasareba
		2. oosiitasimasureba	1. oosininareba
		2. oosimohsimasureba	2. oosinasaimasureba
			2. oosininarimasureba
			2. oosiasobaseba
			3. oosiasobasimasureba
pres. neg.	osaneba	1. osimasenkereba	1. oosinasaraneba
		2. oosiitasimaseneba	1. oosininaraneba
		2. oosimohsimaseneba	1. oosinasarankereba
			2. oosinasaimaseneba
			2. oosininarimasenkereba
			2. oosiasobasaneba
			3. oosiasobasimasenkereba

(-seneba or -senkereba, alternative)

pas. pos.	ositara	1. osimasitara (ba)	1. oosinasattara(ba)
		2. oosiitasimasitara(ba)	1. oosininattara(ba)
		2. oosimohsimasitara (ba)	2. oosinasaimasitara(ba)
			2. oosininarimasitara(ba)
			2. oosiasobasitara(ba)
			3. oosiasobasimasitara(ba)

pas. neg.	osanandara		
		1. osimasendesitara (ba)	1. oosinasaranandara(ba)
		2. oosiitasimasendesitara(ba)	1. oosinasaranakattara(ba)
		2. oosimohsimasendesitara (ba)	1. oosininaranandara(ba)
			1. oosininaranakattara(ba)
			2. oosinasaimasendesitara(ba)
			2. oosininarimasendesitara(ba)
			2. oosiasobasanandara(ba)
			2. oosiasobasanakattara(ba)
			3. oosiasobasimasendesitara(ba)

fut. pos.	osohnaraba		
		1. osimasyohnara (ba)	1. oosinasarohnara(ba)
		2. oosiitasimasyohnara(ba)	1. oosininarohnara(ba)
		2. oosimohsimasyohnara(ba)	2. oosinasaimasyohnara(ba)
			2. oosininarimasyohnara(ba)
			2. oosiasobasohnara(ba)
			3. oosiasobasimasyohnara(ba)

fut. neg.	osumainaraba		
		1. osimasumainara (ba)	1. oosinasarumainara(ba)
		2. oosiitasimasumainara (ba)	1. oosininarumainara(ba)
		2. oosimohsimasumainara(ba)	2. oosinasaimasumainara(ba)
			2. oosininarimasumainara(ba)
			2. oosiasobasumainara(ba)
			3. oosiasobasimasumainara(ba)

JAPANESE VERBS DEFINED IN ENGLISH
Continued from previous page (lower section)

tire.

Hikitukeru (7 en) to attract, draw; to charm; to be convulsed.

Hikitureru (7 ex) to accompany.

Hikiukeru (7 ex) to accept; to guarantee; to assume responsibility.

Hikiwaru (6 ex) to grind, saw.

Hikiwatasu (8 ex) to hand over, deliver; to stretch across.

Hikiyoseru (7 ex) to draw toward one; to attract, draw.

Hikizuru (6 ex) to drag, to shuffle.

Hikkaburu (6 ex) to pull over one's head.

Hikkakaru (6 en) to get caught, be hooked.

Hikkakeru (7 ex) to hook, hang, hitch; to seduce, cheat.

Hikkaku (3 ex) to scratch, claw.

Hikkarageru (7 ex) to tuck up, bundle, bind.

Hikkomasu (8 ex) to withdraw, pull in, take back.

Hikkomeru (7 ex) same as **Hikkomasu.**

Hikkomu (4 en) to retract, retire; same as **Hikikomu.**

Hikkonuku (3 ex) same as **Hikinuku.**

Hikkosu (8 en) to remove to.

Continued on next page (lower section)

IMPERATIVE

pos.	ose		1. oosinasai 2. oosinasaimase 2. oosiasobase 3. oosiasobasimase
neg.	osuna		1. oosinasaruna 2. oosinasaimasuna 2. oosiasobasuna 3. oosiasobasimasuna

ADJECTIVE

pos.	osu	1. osimasu(ru) 2. oosiitasimasu(ru) 2. oosimohsimasu(ru)	1. oosinasaru 1. oosininaru 2. oosinasaimasu(ru) 2. oosininarimasu(ru) 2. oosiasobasu 3. oosiasobasimasu(ru)
neg.	osanu	1. osimasen(u) 2. oosiitasimasen(u) 2. oosimohsimasen(u)	1. oosinasaran(u)(ai) 1. oosininaran(u)(ai) 2. oosinasaimasen(u) 2. oosininarimasen(u) 2. oosiasobasan(u) 3. oosiasobasimasen(u)

CONJUNCTIVE

pos.	osite	1. osimasite 2. oosiitasimasite 2. oosimohsimasite	1. oosinasatte 1. oosininatte 2. oosinasaimasite 2. oosininarimasite 2. oosiasobasite 3. oosiasobasimasite
neg.	osanaide	1. osimasende(site) 2. oosiitasimasende(site) 2. oosimohsimasende(site)	1. oosinarasaranaide 1. oosininaranaide 2. oosinasaimasende(site) 2. oosininarimasende(site) 2. oosiasobasanaide 3. oosiasobasimasenda(site)

(-naide or -nakutte, alternative)

CONNECTIVE

osi-

SUBSTANTIVE

osi

JAPANESE VERBS DEFINED IN ENGLISH
Continued from previous page (lower section)

Hikkurikaeru (6 en) to turn turtle, be overturned, tumble down.

Hikkurikaesu (8 ex) to upset, turn upside down, overturn; to turn inside out; to mess about.

Hiku (3 ex) to draw, pull, haul, tow, tug, drag; to saw, grind; to attract, quote; to consult (a dicionary); to subtract; to play a musical instrument; to run over.

Hiku (3 en) to resign; to fall back, retreat, lessen, sink, fall, diminish.

Hinekureru (7 en) to be crooked, distorted, twisted; to be eccentric.

Hineru (6 ex) to nip, twiddle, twist, wrench, wring.

Hipparu (6 ex) to pull, draw, tug, drag; to stretch over, strain; to postpone, defer.

Hirakeru (7 en) to open; to become civilized.

Hiraku (3 ex) to open; to lay open; to start.

Hiraku (3 en) to open.

Hiramekasu (8 ex) to flash, flourish.

Hirameku (3 en) to sparkle, glitter, flash.

Hirehusu (8 en) to prostrate oneself.

Hirogaru (6 en) to expand, stretch, spread, widen.

Hirogeru (7 ex) to enlarge,

Continued on next page (lower section)

THE VERBS OF THE EIGHTH CONJUGATION

More than ten per cent of all Japanese verbs belong to this conjugation. The ending **su** is probably derived from the verb **suru, sasu, saseru** (to do, to let do), which may be the reason why all verbs of this conjugation are exo-active.

arasu, to ransack.
hitasu, to steep.
ikasu, to let live.
kaesu, to return.
kasu, to lend.
kesu, to extinguish.
kogasu, to scorch.
kuzusu, to crush.
mesu, to call.
modosu, to return.

musu, to steam.
nobasu, to extend.
otosu, to drop.
sagasu, to search.
sasu, to pierce.
taosu, to fell.
terasu, to illuminate.
tubusu, to demolish.
utsusu, to transfer.
yosu, to assemble.

Some of the verbs ending in -su have variant form ending in **-seru,** in which case they belong to the 7th conjugation, thus:

> **kasu or kaseru,** to lend.
> **yosu or yoseru,** to assemble.
> **kuwasu or kuwaseru,** to let eat.
> **awasu or awaseru,** to let meet, to mix.
> **miawasu or miawaseru,** to put off, to postpone.
> **makasu or makaseru,** to give in charge of, to trust.
> **yowasu or yowaseru,** to make intoxicated.
> **kawasu or kawaseru,** to let buy.

JAPANESE VERBS DEFINED IN ENGLISH
Continued from previous page (lower section)

broaden, spread, widen, extend; to unfold, open, outspread.

Hiroiageru (7 ex) to pick up.

Hiroidasu (8 ex) to pick out, select.

Hiromaru (6 en) to spread, circulate; to be in fashion.

Hiromeru (7 ex) to extend, widen, broaden; to diffuse, spread, propagate.

Hirou (10 ex) to pick up, gather, glean; to select, pick out.

Hiru (7 en) to dry, ebb.

Hirugaeru (6 en) to turn over; to stream, float, wave.

Hirugaesu (8 ex) to turn over; to fly, wave.

Hirumu (4 en) to waver, flinch, shrink from fear.

Hisagu (2 ex) to sell, deal in, trade.

Hisigeru (7 en) to be crushed.

Hisigu (2 ex) to crush.

Hisimeku (3 en) to push about; to make an uproar.

Hisomeru (7 ex) to lower, subdue; to hide, conceal; to knit brows.

Hisomu (4 en) to lurk, be latent, hide, conceal onself.

Hissageru (7 ex) to carry, take along with.

Hisuru (11b ex) to compare, match; to hide, keep secret.

Hitasu (8 ex) to soak, steep, immerse, dip.

Hittakuru (6 ex) to snatch.

Hittateru (7 ex) same as **Hikitateru.**

Hittuku (3 en) to stick to, adhere to.

Hiyakasu (8 ex) to ridicule, joke, rally, make fun of.

Hizamaduku (3 en) to kneel, genuflect; fall on one's knees.

Hizumu (4 en) to be bent, be

Continued on next page (lower section)

THE NINTH CONJUGATION (a)

INDICATIVE

pres. pos.	matu	waits
pres. neg.	matan	does not wait
pas. pos.	matta	did wait
pas. neg.	matananda	did not wait
fut. pos.	matoh	will wait
fut. neg.	matumai	will not wait
fut. pas. pos.	mattaroh	will have waited
fut. pas. neg.	matanandaroh	will not have waited

CONDITIONAL

pres. pos.	mateba	if waits
pres. neg.	mataneba	if does not wait
pas. pos.	mattara	if did wait
pas. neg	matanandara	if did not wait
fut. pos.	matohnaraba	if would wait
fut. neg.	matumainaraba	if would not wait

IMPERATIVE

pos.	mate	wait!
neg.	matuna	do not wait!

ADJECTIVAL

pos.	matu	waiting
neg.	matanu	not waiting

CONJUNCTIVE

pos.	matte	waits and
neg.	matanaide	waits not and

CONNECTIVE

mati-	....

SUBSTANTIVE

mati	waiting

INTERROGATIVE

JAPANESE VERBS DEFINED IN ENGLISH
Continued from previous page (lower section)

crooked, be warped.

Hodokeru (7 en) to get loose.

Hodokosu (8 ex) to give alms; to apply.

Hodoku (3 ex) to untie, unbind, unfasten.

Hoeru (7 en) to bark, bay, cry.

Hohmuru (6 ex) to bury, entomb, inter.

Hohridasu (8 ex) to throw up.

Hohru (6 ex) to throw, cast, pitch, fling; to give up, abandon. cast out, dump.

Hohrikomu (4 ex) to throw into, cast into.

Hohzuru (7a or 11b ex) to report, inform, announce; to repay, revenge; to dedicate; to obey, ob-

Continued on next page (lower section)

Peace Memorial Park

Tokyo Tower

THE NINTH CONJUGATION (b)

	PART I (all persons)	PART II (1st & 3rd persons)	PART III (2nd person)
INDICATIVE			
pres. pos.	matu	1. matimasu 2. omatiitasimasu 2. omatimohsimasu	1. omatinasaru 1. omatininaru 2. omatinasaimasu 2. omatininarimasu 2. omatiasobasu 3. omatiasobasimasu
pres. neg.	matan(ai)	1. matimasen 2. omatiitasimasen 2. omatimohsimasen	1. omatinasaran(ai) 1. omatininaran(ai) 2. omatinasaimasen 2. omatininarimasen 2. omatiasobasan(ai) 3. omatiasobasimasen
pas. pos.	matta	1. matimasita 2. omatiitasimasita 2. omatimohsimasita	1. omatinasatta 1. omatininatta 2. omatinasaimasita 2. omatiasobasita 3. omatiasobasimasita
pas. neg.	matananda matanakatta	1. matimasendesita 2. omatiitasimasendesita 2. omatimohsimasendesita	1. omatinasarananda 1. omatininarananda 1. omatinasaranakatta 1. omatininaranakatta 2. omatinasaimasendesita 2. omatininarimasendesita 2. omatiasobasananda 2. omatiasobasanakatta 3. omatiasobasimasendesita
fut. pos.	matoh	1. matimasyoh 2. omatiitasimasyoh 2. omatimohsimasyoh	1. omatinasaroh 1. omatininaroh 2. omatinasaimasyoh 2. omatininarimasyoh 3. omatiasobasimasyoh
fut. neg.	matumai	1. matimasumai 2. omatiitasimasumai 2. omatimohsimasumai	1. omatinasarumai 1. omatininarumai 2. omatinasaimasumai 2. omatininarimasumai 2. omatiasobasumai 3. omatiasobasimasumai
fut. pas. pas.	mattaroh	1. matimasitaroh 2. omatiitasimasitaroh 2. omatimohsimasitaroh	1. omatinasattaroh 1. omatininattaroh 2. omatinasaimasitaroh 2. omatininarimasitaroh 2. omatiasobasitaroh 3. omatiasobasimasitaroh (-taroh or -tadesyoh, alternative)
fut. pas. neg.	matanadaroh	1. matimasendesitaroh 2. omatinasaimasendesitaroh 2. omatimohsimasendesitaroh	1. omatinasaranandaroh 1. omatininaranandaroh 1. omatinasaranakattaroh 1. omatininaranakattaroh 2. omatinasaimasendesitaroh 2. omatininarimasendesitaroh 2. omatiasobasanandaroh 2. omatiasobasanakattaroh 3. omatiasobasimasendesitaroh (-daroh or -dadesyoh, alternative)

JAPANESE VERBS DEFINED IN ENGLISH
Continued from previous page (lower section)

serve, follow; to die, pass away. bellow, howl, roar.

Hokoru (6 en) to boast, brag; to be proud of.

Hokorobiru (7 en) to be rent, rip; to burst open, bloom.

Homeru (7 ex) to praise, admire, applaud, commend.

Honeoru (6 en) to labor, toil, struggle.

Continued on next page (lower section)

CONDITIONAL

pres. pos.	mateba	1. omatinasareba
	1. matimasureba	1. omatininareba
	2. omatiitasimasureba	2. omatinasaimasureba
	2. omatimohsimasureba	2. omatininarimasureba
		2. omatiasobaseba
		3. omatiasobasimasureba
pres. neg.	mataneba	1. omatinasaraneba
	1. matimasenkereba	1. omatininaraneba
	2. omatiitasimaseneba	1. omatinasarankereba
	2. omatimohsimaseneba	2. omatinasaimasenebe
		2. omatininarimasenkereba
		2. omatiasobasaneba
		3. omatiasobasimasenkereba

(-seneba or -senkereba, alternative)

past. pos.	mattara	1. omatinasattara(ba)
	1. matimasitara(ba)	1. omatininattara(ba)
	2. omatiitasimasitara(ba)	2. omatinasaimasitara(ba)
	2. omatimohsimasitara(ba)	2. omatininarimasitara(ba)
		2. omatiasobasitara(ba)
		3. omatiasobasimasitara(ba)
pas. neg.	matanandara	1. omatinasaranandara(ba)
	1. matimasendesitara(ba)	1. omatinasaranakattara(ba)
	2. omatiitasimasendesitara(ba)	1. omatininaranandara(ba)
	2. omatimohsimasendesitara(ba)	1. omatininaranakattara(ba)
		2. omatinasaimasendesitara(ba)
		2. omatininarimasendesitara(ba)
		2. omatiasobasanandara(ba)
		2. omatiasobasanakattara(ba)
		3. omatiasobasimasendesitara(ba)
fut. pos.	matohnaraba	1. omatinasarohnara(ba)
	1. matimasyohnara(ba)	1. omatininarohnara(ba)
	2. omatiitasimasyohnara(ba)	2. omatinasaimasyohnara(ba)
	2. omatimohsimasyohnara(ba)	2. omatininarimasyohnara(ba)
		2. omatiasobasohnara(ba)
		3. omatiasobasimasyohnara(ba)
fut. neg.	matumainara(ba)	1. omatinasarumainara(ba)
	1. matimasumainara(ba)	2. omatininarimasumainara(ba)
	2. omatiitasimasumainara(ba)	1. omatininarumainara(ba)
	2. omatimohsimasumainara(ba)	2. omatinasaimasumainara(ba)
		2. omatiasobasumainara(ba)
		3. omatiasobasimasumainara(ba)

JAPANESE VERBS DEFINED IN ENGLISH
Continued from previous page (lower section)

Honomekasu (8 en) to hint, suggest.

Honomeku (3 en) to appear faintly; to shine dimly; to be hinted.

Horeru (7 en) to be fascinated, enamored; be in love with.

Horidasu (8 ex) to dig out, unearth, exhume.

Horu (6 ex) to dig, cut, excavate, scoop, hollow out; to inquire into, probe, search; to carve, engrave, chisel, inscribe; to tattoo.

Hosigaru (6 en) to desire, wish for, long for, covet.

Hosomeru (7 ex) to make fine, thin, slender, narrow.

Hosoru (6 en) to become small, dwindle.

Hossuru (11b ex) to desire, wish, want; to intend, purpose, will.

Hosu (8 ex) to dry, desiccate.

Hottirakasu (8 ex) to neglect, disregard.

Hotureru (7 en) to loosen, become loose, ravel, be frayed.

Hottarakasu (8 ex) to neglect, disregard, leave alone. (Same as hottirakasu).

Hozikuru (6 ex) to dig up, pick, scratch.

Hyohsuru (11b ex) to criticize, estimate; to express, show.

Hueru (7 en) to increase, multiply, accrue.

Huhziru (7 ex) to seal, enclose; to blockade.

Hukasu (8 ex) to puff, smoke;

Continued on next page (lower section)

IMPERATIVE

pos.	mate		1. omatinasai
			2. omatinasaimase
			2. omatiasobase
			3. omatiasobasimase
neg.	matuna		1. omatinasaruna
			2. omatinasaimasuna
			2. omatiasobasuna
			3. omatiasobasimasuna

ADJECTIVE

pos.	matu		1. omatinasaru
		1. matimasu (ru)	1. omatininaru
		2. omatiitasimasu (ru)	2. omatinasaimasu (ru)
		2. omatimohsimasu (ru)	2. omatininarimasu (ru)
			2. omatiasobasu
			3. omatiasobasimasu (ru)
neg.	matanu		1. omatinasaran (u) (ai)
		1. matimasen (u)	1. omatininaran (u) (ai)
		2. omatiitasimasen (u)	2. omatinasaimasen (u)
		2. omatimohsimasen (u)	2. omatininarimasen (u)
			2. omatiasobasan (u) (ai)
			3. omatiasobasimasen (u)

CONJUNCTIVE

pos.	matte		1. omatinasatte
		1. matimasite	1. omatininatte
		2. omatiitasimasite	2. omatinasaimasite
		2. omatimohsimasite	2. omatininarimasite
			2. omatiasobasite
			3. omatiasobasimasite
neg.	matanaide		1. omatinasaranaide
		1. matimasende (site)	1. omatininaranaide
		2. omatiitasimasende (site)	2. omatinasaimasende (site)
		2. omatimohsimasende (site)	2. omatininarimasende (site)
			2. omatiasobasanaide
			3. omatiasobasimasende (site)

(-naide or -nakutte, alternative)

CONNECTIVE   mati-

SUBSTANTIVE   mati

JAPANESE VERBS DEFINED IN ENGLISH

Continued from previous page (lower section)

to sit up late; to steam.

Hukeru (7 en) to grow late.

Hukeru (6 en) to be addicted to, indulge in, be given to.

Hukitirasu (8 ex) to blow off, scatter.

Hukidasu (8 ex) to spout, gush, blow, erupt, spurt.

Hukideru (7 en) to spout, blow, erupt.

Hukikaesu (8 en) to blow over; to come to oneself.

Hukikesu (8 ex) to blow out, extinguish.

Hukikomu (4 ex) to blow in, blow into; to wipe and polish.

Hukimodosu (8 ex) to blow back.

Hukinuku (3 ex) to blow through.

Hukitobasu (8 ex) to mop off.

Hukitoru (6 ex) to mop off, wipe away.

Hukitukeru (7 ex) to blow against.

Hukiwakeru (7 ex) to winnow; to smelt; to assay.

Huku (3 ex) to blow, spout, erupt, emit; to breathe out; to wipe; to cover, thatch, tile.

Hukumeru (7 ex) to include, put into; to give private instructions, give an understanding.

Hukumu (4 en) to hold in one's mouth; to bear in mind; to hold, contain.

Hukuramu (4 en) to bulge, swell out, distend.

Hukuramasu (8 ex) to inflate, expand, make swell.

Continued on next page (lower section)

THE VERBS OF THE NINTH CONJUGATION

Exo-active verbs	Endo-active verbs
hanatu, to let go.	ayamatu, to make a mistake.
motu, to have.	kakotu, to lament.
nageutu, to throw.	katu, to win.
tamotu, to hold.	motu, to keep.
tatu, to cut.	sobadatu, to stand high.
ugatu, to dig.	sodatu, to thrive.
utu, to strike.	tatu, to stand.
wakatu, to divide.	

The above is nearly all the verbs belonging to this conjugation.

JAPANESE VERBS DEFINED IN ENGLISH

Continued from previous page (lower section)

Hukurakasu (8 ex) same as **hukuramasu**.

Hukurasu (8 ex) to swell, expand, inflate, puff off.

Hukureru (7 en) to swell, bulge, bag, puff off.

Hukusuru (11b en) to obey, submit to; to be restored to; to return to.

Humidasu (8 en) to step forward, to start.

Humihazusu (8 en) to miss one's foot.

Humikatameru (7 ex) to stamp down.

Humikoeru (7 ex) to step over.

Humikomu (4 en) to step into.

Humikorosu (8 ex) to trample to death.

Humikotaeru (7 en) to hold out, stand firm, keep one's ground.

Humimayou (10 en) to stray, wander, lose one's way.

Huminarasu (8 ex) to read down, beat; to make a squeak by treading.

Huminiziru (6 ex) to trample under foot.

Humisimeru (7 en) to step firmly.

Humitaosu (8 ex) to trample down.

Humitodomaru (6 en) to make a stand, hold one's ground.

Humitubusu (8 ex)·to smash by treading.

Humu (4 ex) to tread on, stamp on; to step, walk; to keep, make good, fulfill.

Hunbaru (6 en) to stride, straddle; to insist on, hold fast to.

Hurareru (7 en) to be rejected.

Hurasu (8 ex) to make fall.

Hureru (7 en) to shake, swing; to touch; to conflict with; to proclaim.

Huridasu (8 ex) to shake out, throw; to begin to rain.

Hurikaeru (6 en) to turn one's head, turn around, look back; to transfer, change.

Hurikakeru (7 ex) to sprinkle.

Hurimawasu (8 ex) to swing, flourish, wield.

Huriotosu (8 ex) to spill, shake off.

Hurisikiru (6 en) to rain incessantly.

Hurisuteru (7 ex) to shake off; to abandon; to disdain.

Huru (6 en) to fall, come down, rain; to wag, wave, shake; to reject.

Hurubiru (7 en) to age, look old, have been service.

Hurueru (7 en) to shake, tremble, quiver.

Huruidasu (8 en) to begin to tremble.

Huruidasu (8 ex) to throw out, weed out, sieve out.

Huruiotosu (8 ex) to shake off.

Huruiwakeru (7 ex) to sift, winnow, bolt; to select.

Hurumau (10 en) to behave oneself, act, conduct oneself.

Continued on next page (lower section)

THE TENTH CONJUGATION (a)

INDICATIVE

pres. pos.	arau	washes
pres. neg.	arawan	does not wash
pas. pos.	aratta	did wash
pas. neg.	arawananda	did not wash
fut. pos.	araoh	will wash
fut. neg.	araumai	will not wash
fut. pas. pos.	arattaroh	will have washed
fut. pas. neg.	arawanandaroh	will not have washed

CONDITIONAL

pres. pos.	araeba	if washes
pres. neg.	arawaneba	if does not wash
pas. pos.	arattara	if did wash
pas. neg.	arawanandara	if did not wash
fut. pos.	araohnaraba	if would wash
fut. neg.	araumainaraba	if would not wash

IMPERATIVE

pos.	arae	wash!
neg.	arauna	do not wash!

ADJECTIVAL

pos.	arau	washing
neg.	arawanu	not washing

CONJUNCTIVE

pos.	aratte	washes and
neg.	arawanaide	washes not and

CONNECTIVE

	arai-	--------------

SUBSTANTIVE

	arai	washing

INTERROGATIVE

JAPANESE VERBS DEFINED IN ENGLISH
Continued from previous page (lower section)

Huruu (10 en) to tremble, shake.

Huruu (10 ex) to sift, sieve, bolt, shake.

Husagaru (6 en) to choke, clog, be blocked.

Husagikomu (4 en) to be in low spirits, be gloom, be melancholy.

Husagu (2 ex) to block, choke, clog, stop, obstruct, shut, plug.

Husagu (2 en) to be melancholy, have blues, be in low spirits.

Husaru (6 en) to lie face down.

Husegu (2 ex) to prevent, guard against; to defend, resist, check.

Huseru (7 ex) to invert, turn down, reverse.

Huseru (6 en) to go to bed, to lie down.

Husu (8 en) to lie down.

Husuberu (7 ex) to fumigate, smoke, cure.

Husuboru (6 en) to be smoky, smoke.

Husuburu (6 en) to smoke, be smoky.

Huhsuru (11b en) to suggest, hint.

Hutoru (6 en) to grow fat, fatten, become fleshy.

Huyakasu (8 ex) to soak, steep.

Huyakeru (7 en) to grow sodden.

Huyasu (8 ex) to increase, mul-

Continued on next page (lower section)

THE TENTH CONJUGATION (b)

	PART I (all persons)	PART II (1st & 3rd persons)	PART III (2nd person)
INDICATIVE			
pres. pos.	arau	1. araimasu 2. oaraiitasimasu 2. oaraimohsimasu	1. oarainasaru 1. oaraininaru 2. oarainasaimasu 2. oaraininarimasu 2. oaraiasobasu 3. oaraiasobasimasu
pres. neg.	arawan(ai)	1. araimasen 2. oaraiitasimasen 2. oaraimohsimasen	1. oarainasaran(ai) 1. oaraininaran(ai) 2. oarainasaimasen 2. oaraininarimasen 2. oaraiasobasan(ai) 3. oaraiasobasimasen
pas. pos.	aratta arohta	1. araimasita 2. oaraiitasimasita 2. oaraimohsimasita	1. oarainasatta 1. oaraininatta 2. oarainasaimasita 2. oaraininarimasita 2. oaraiasobasita 3. oaraiasobasimasita
pas. neg.	arawananda arawanakatta	1. araimasendesita 2. oaraiitasimasendesita 2. oaraimohsimasendesita	1. oarainasarananda 1. oaraininarananda 1. oarainasaranakatta 1. oaraininaranakatta 2. oarainasaimasendesita 2. oaraininarimasendesita 2. oaraiasobasananda 2. oaraiasobasanakatta 3. oaraiasobasimasendesita
fut. pos.	arawananda	1. araimasyoh 2. oaraiitasimasyoh 2. oaraimohsimasyoh	1. oarainasaroh 1. oaraininaroh 2. oarainasaimasyoh 2. oaraininarimasyoh 3. oaraiasobasimasyoh
fut. neg.	araumai	1. araimasumai 2. oaraiitasimasumai 2. oaraimohsimasumai	1. oarainasarumai 1. oaraininarumai 2. oarainasaimasumai 2. oaraininarimasumai 2. oaraiasobasumai
futu. pas. pos.	arattaroh	1. araimasitaroh 2. oaraiitasimasitaroh 2. oaraimohsimasitaroh	1. oarainasattaroh 1. oaraininattaroh 2. oarainasaimasitaroh 2. oaraininarimasitaroh 2. oaraiasobasitaroh 3. oaraiasobasimasitaroh
		(-taroh or -tadesyoh, alternative)	
fut. pas. neg.	arawanandaroh arawanakattaroh	1. araimasendesitaroh 2. oaraiitasimasendesitaroh 2. oaraimohsimasendesitaroh	1. oarainasaranandaroh 1. oarainasaranakattaroh 1. oaraininaranandaroh 1. oaraininaranakattaroh 2. oarainasaimasendesitaroh 2. oaraininarimasendesitaroh 2. oaraiasobasanandaroh 2. oaraiasobasanakattaroh 3. oaraiasobasimasendesitaroh
		(-daroh or -dadesyoh, alternative)	

JAPANESE VERBS DEFINED IN ENGLISH

Continued from previous page (lower section)

tiply.

Huzakeru (7 en) to flirt, coquet; to romp, sport, frolic, jest, joke.

Iawasu (8 en) to happen to be present, be present by chance.

Ibaru (6 en) to be haughty, domineer, swagger, be stuck up.

Ibiru (6 ex) to tease, annoy,

Continued on next page (lower section)

CONDITIONAL

pres. pos.	araeba	1. oarainasareba
	1. araimasureba	1. oaraininareba
	2. oaralitasimasureba	2. oarainasaimasureba
	2. oaraimohsimasureba	2. oaraininarimasureba
		2. oaraiasobaseba
		3. oaraiasobasimasureba
pres. neg.	arawaneba	1. oarainasaraneba
	1. araimasenkereba	1. oaraininaraneba
	2. oaralitasimaseneba	1. oaraininarankereba
	2. oaraimohsimaseneba	2. oarainasaimaseneba
		2. oaraininarimasenkereba
		2. oaraiasobasaneba
		3. oaraiasobasimasenkereba

(-seneba or -senkereba, alternative)

pas. pos.	arattara(ba)	1. oarainasattara(ba)
	1. araimasitara(ba)	1. oaraininattara(ba)
	2. oaralitasimasitara(ba)	2. oarainasaimasitara(ba)
	2. oaraimohsimasitara(ba)	2. oaraininarimasitara(ba)
		2. oaraiasobasitara(ba)
		3. oaraiasobasimasitara(ba)
pas. neg.	arawanandara(ba)	1. oaraininaranandara(ba)
	arawanakattara(ba)	1. oarainasaranandara(ba)
	1. araimasendesitara(ba)	1. oarainasaranakattara(ba)
	2. oaralitasimasendesitara(ba)	1. oaraininaranakattara(ba)
	2. oaraimohsimasendesitara(ba)	2. oarainasaimasendesitara(ba)
		2. oaraininarimasendesitara(ba)
		2. oarIasobasanandara(ba)
		2. oaraiasobasanakattara(ba)
		3. oaraiasobasimasendesitara(ba)
fut. pos.	araohnara(ba)	1. oarainasarohnara(ba)
	1. araimasyohnara(ba)	1. oaraininarohnara(ba)
	2. oaralitasimasyohnara(ba)	2. oarainasaimasyohnara(ba)
	2. oaraimohsimaysyohnara(ba)	2. oaraininarimasyohnara(ba)
		2. oaraiasobasohnara(ba)
		3. oaraiasobasimasyohnara(ba)
fut. neg.	araumainara(ba)	1. oarainasarumainara(ba)
	1. araimasumainara(ba)	1. oaraininarumainara(ba)
	2. oaralitasimasumainara(ba)	2. oarainasaimasumainara(ba)
	2. oaraimohsimasumainara(ba)	2. oaraininarimasumainara(ba)
		2. oaraiasobasumainara(ba)
		3. oaraiasobasimasumainara(ba)

JAPANESE VERBS DEFINED IN ENGLISH
Continued from previous page (lower section)

torment.

Ikubaru (6 en) to doubt, suspect, wonder, marvel.

Iburu (6 en) to smoke, smoulder.

Ibusu (8 ex) to smoke, make smoky, fumigate.

Idaku (3 ex) to hold in arms, to hug; to cherish, harbor, entertain. (usually **daku**).

Idasu (8 ex) to take out, bring forth; to produce, yield. (usually **dasu**).

Idomu (4 ex) to challenge, defy, dare, provoke; to entice.

Iiateru (7 ex) to prophesy; to guess.

Iidasu (8 en) to begin to speak, start to talk; to utter, speak out.

Iihukumeru (7 en) to instruct,

inculcate.

Iihurasu (8 en) to make public, spread.

Iihuseru (7 ex) to silence, comfute.

Iiharu (6 en) to insist on, persist in, assert, maintain.

Iikaeru (7 en) to say in other words.

Iikaesu (8 en) to answer back, retort.

Iikakeru (7 en) to begin to speak; to address, accost; to accuse.

Iikaneru (7 en) to hesitate to say.

Iikawasu (8 en) to promise mutually.

Iikikasu (8 ex) to instruct, tell;

Continued on next page (lower section)

IMPERATIVE

(addressed to 2d person only)

pos.	arae		1. oarainasai
			2. oarainasaimase
			2. oaraiasobase
			3. oaraiasobasimase
neg.	arauna		1. oarainasaruna
			2. oarainasaimasuna
			2. oaraiasobasuna
			3. oaraiasobasimasuna

ADJECTIVE

pos.	arau		1. oarainasaru
		1. araimasu(ru)	1. oaraininaru
		2. oaraiitasimasu(ru)	2. oarainasaimasu(ru)
		2. oaraimohsimasu(ru)	2. oaraininarimasu(ru)
			2. oaraiasobasu
			3. oaraiasobasimasu(ru)
neg.	arawan(u)(ai)		1. oarainasaran(u)(ai)
		1. araimasen(u)	1. oaraininaran(u)(ai)
		2. oaraiitasimasen(u)	2. oarainasaimasen(u)
		2. oaraimohsimasen(u)	2. oaraininarimasen(u)
			2. oaraiasobasan(u)(ai)
			3. oaraiasobasimasen(u)

CONJUNCTIVE

pos.	aratte		1. oarainasatte
	arohte		1. oaraininatte
		1. araimasite	2. oarainasaimasite
		2. oaraiitasimasite	2. oaraininarimasite
		2. oaraimohsimasite	2. oaraiasobasite
			3. oaraiasobasimasite
neg.	arawande		1. oarainasaranaide
	arawanaide		1. oaraininaranaide
	arawanakutte		2. oarainasaimasende(site)
		1. araimasende(site)	2. oaraininarimasende(site)
		2. oaraiitasimasende(site)	2. oaraiasobasanaide
		2. oaraimohsimasende(site)	3. oaraiasobasimasende(site)
			(-naide or -nakutte, alternative)

CONNECTIVE

arai-

SUBSTANTIVE

arai

JAPANESE VERBS DEFINED IN ENGLISH
Continued from previous page (lower section)

to admonish.

Iikiru (6 en) to finish saying; to declare, assert.

Iikomeru (7 ex) to talk down, silence.

Iikurumeru (7 ex) to dupe, argue into consent.

Iinareru (7 en) to become used to say.

Iisugiru (7 en) to speak too much.

Iiitasu (8 en) to say in addition.

Iitukeru (7 en) to order, command, direct.

Iiyoru (6 en) to court, woo.

Ikaru (6 en) to be angry, be offended, lose patience.

Ikedoru (6 ex) to catch, capture, catch alive; to take prisoner.

Ikeru (7 ex) to set flowers; to keep alive.

Ikidohru (6 en) to be indignant, resent, be angry, be enraged.

Ikikaeru (6 en) to return to life, revive.

Ikinobiru (7 en) to survive, outlive.

Ikiru (7 en) to live; to revive.

Ikomu (4 en) to shoot into; to cast.

Ikou (10 en) to take a rest.

Imasimeru (7 ex) to caution, warn; to forbid, prohibit.

Imu (4 ex) to dislike, abhor, loathe; to avoid, shun.

Inamu (4 ex) to decline; to refuse, deny.

Inanaku (3 en) to neigh.

Inoru (6 en) to pray, supplicate; to imprecate; to wish.

Inuru (11c en) to go home, return.

Continued on next page (lower section)

Wish Tree-Heian Jingu Shrine

Buddha

THE VERBS OF THE TENTH CONJUGATION

About ten per cent of all the Japanese verbs belong to this conjugation. The following are therefore only a part of them.

Exo-active verbs	Endo-active verbs
harau, to pay.	au, to meet.
huruu, to shake.	deau, to meet together
kakou, to enclose.	hau, to crawl.
kamau, to mind.	huruu, to tremble.
kau, to buy.	ikou, to repose.
hirou, to pick up.	kanau, to match.
iu, to say.	kuruu, to be crazy.
iwau, to celebrate.	mukau, to oppose.
negau, to wish.	niou, to smell.
nuu, to sew.	sorou, to be arranged.
tikau, to pledge.	sumau, to reside.
utau, to sing.	uruu, to be moist.

In the primary conjugation marked in the table as I (for all persons), the verbs of this conjugation have two forms in the indicative past; namely, those ending in -au may end in -atta or ohta, those ending in -ou may have otta or ohta, those ending in -iu may have -itta or -iuta, those ending in -uu may have either -utta or -uuta. For example:

```
utau, to sing. ............................utatta or utohta, sang.
hirou, to pick up. ..................hirotta or hirohta, picked up.
iu, to say. ................................itta or iuta, said.
kuu, to eat. ............................kutta or kuuta, ate.
```

JAPANESE VERBS DEFINED IN ENGLISH
Continued from previous page (lower section)

Irassyaru (6 en) to be (courteous expression), to go; to come.

Ireru (7 ex) to put in, insert; to admit, let in; to accept, listen.

Irikomu (4 en) to enter.

Irikumu (4 en) to be complicated.

Irodaru (6 ex) to color, paint, decorate.

Isameru (7 ex) to remonstrate with; to expostulate with, exhort.

Isamu (4 en) to be inspired with courage, be gallant, be emboldened, be excited.

Isogasu (8 ex) to hasten, hurry up.

Isogu (2 en) to make haste, hasten, hurry, be in a hurry.

Isosimu (4 en) to work diligently.

Issuru (11b ex) to miss; to let slip, let escape.

Isuru (11b ex) to cure, apply remedy.

Itadaku (3 ex) to put on; to receive, accept (ct. exp.); to take, to eat (ct. exp.)

Itagaru (6 en) to complain of pain.

Itameru (7 ex) to injure, harm, hurt.

Itamu (4 en) to hurt, be painful, ache; to be injured, damaged; to grieve, lament.

Itaru (6 en) to go, proceed; to arrive at, reach.

Itasu (8 ex) to do, render (ct. exp.)

Itawaru (6 ex) to pity, sympathize.

Itonamu (4 ex) to do, make; to carry on, conduct, engage in, practice, pursue, perform.

Itou (10 ex) to dislike, hate, loathe, grudge.

Ituku (3 en) to be settled in a

Continued on next page (lower section)

THE ELEVENTH A CONJUGATION (a)

INDICATIVE

pres. pos.	kuru	comes
pres. neg.	kon(u)	does not come
pas. pos.	kita	did come
pas. neg.	konanda	did not come
	konakatta	
fut. pos.	koyoh	will come
fut. neg.	kumai	will not come
fut. pas. pos.	kitaroh	will have come
fut. pas. neg.	konandaroh	will not have come
	konakattaroh	

CONDITIONAL

pres. pos.	kureba	if comes
pres. neg.	konakereba	if does not come
pas. pos.	kitara	if did come
pas. neg.	konandara	if did not come
	konakattara	
fut. pos.	koyohnara(ba)	if would come
fut. neg.	kumainara(ba)	if would not come

IMPERATIVE

pos.	koi	come!
neg.	kuna	do not come!
	kuruna	

ADJECTIVAL

pos.	kuru	coming
neg.	konu	not coming

CONJUNCTIVE

pos.	kite	comes and
neg.	konaide	comes not and

JAPANESE VERBS DEFINED IN ENGLISH
Continued from previous page (lower section)

place.

Ituwaru (6 en) to lie; to falsify; to pretend, feign, make believe.

Iu (10 en) to say, speak, talk, utter, express; to name, call.

Iwaeru (7 ex) to tie, bind.

Iwau (10 ex) to celebrate, commemorate; to congratulate.

Iyagaru (6 en) to dislike, hate.

Iyasimu (4 ex) to scorn, despise, disdain.

Iyasu (8 ex) to cure, heal, restore.

Izikeru (7 en) to shrink with fear; to shrug (with cold)

Izikuru (6 ex) to monkey with.

Izimeru (7 ex) to oppress, harass, tease, annoy, persecute.

Iziru (6 ex) to finger, handle, play with.

Kabau (10 ex) to screen, shelter, protect.

Kabiru (7 en) to mold, mildew.

Kaburu (6 ex) to wear, put on.

Kabusaru (6 en) to hang over; to lap over.

Continued on next page (lower section)

THE ELEVENTH A CONJUGATION (b)

PART I (all persons)		PART II (1st & 3rd persons)	PART III (2nd person)

INDICATIVE

pres. pos.   kuru

PART II:
1. mairimasu
1. sanzimasu
2. sanzyohitasimasu

PART III:
1. irassyaru
1. oidenasaru
1. oideninaru
2. irassyaimasu
2. oidenasaimasu
2. oideninarimasu
2. oideasobasu
3. oideasobasimasu

pres. neg.   kon(u)

PART II:
1. mairimasen
1. sanzimasen
2. sanzyohitasimasen

PART III:
1. irassyaran
1. oidenasaran
1. oideninaran
2. irassyaimasen
2. oidenasaimasen
2. oideninarimasen
2. oideasobasan
3. oideasobasimasen

pas. pos.   kita

PART II:
1. mairimasita
1. sanzimasita
2. sanzyohitasimasita

PART III:
1. irassyatta
1. oidenasatta
1. oideninatta
2. irassyaimasita
2. oidenasaimasita
2. oideninarimasita
2. oideasobasita
3. oideasobasimasita

pas. neg.   konanda
konakatta

PART II:
1. mairimasendesita
1. sanzimasendesita
2. sanzyohitasimasendesita

PART III:
1. irassyarananda
1. irassyaranakatta
1. oidenasarananda
1. oidenasaranakatta
2. irassyaimasendesita
2. oidenasaimasendesita
2. oideasobasananda
2. oideasobasanakatta
3. oideasobasimasendesita

fut. pos.   koyoh

PART II:
1. mairimasyoh
1. sanzimasyoh

PART III:
1. irassyaroh
1. oidenasaroh
2. irassyaimasyoh
2. oidenasaimasyoh
2. oideninarimasyoh
2. irassyaimasudesyoh
2. oidenasaimasudesyoh
2. oideninarimasudesyoh
2. oideasobasudesyoh
3. oideasobasimasudesyoh

fut. neg.   kumai

PART II:
1. mairimasumai
1. sanzimasumai

PART III:
1. irassyarumai
1. oidenasarumai
2. irassyaimasumai
2. oidenasaimasumai
2. oideninarimasumai
2. oidenasarandesyoh
2. oideninarandesyoh
2. irassyaimasendesyoh
2. oidenasaimasendesyoh
2. oideninarimasendesyoh
2. oideasobasumai
2. oideasobasandesyoh
2. oideasobasimasumai
3. oideasobasimasendesyoh

JAPANESE VERBS DEFINED IN ENGLISH
Continued from previous page (lower section)

Kabuseru (7 ex) to cover, put over; to over-lay; to dash on; to pour on.

Kadukeru (7 ex) to pretend, make an excuse by.

Katihokoru (6 en) to be tri-

Continued on next page (lower section)

		Column A	Column B
fut. pas. pos.	**kitaroh**	1. mairimasitaroh 1. saizimasitaroh 2. mairimasitadesyoh 2. sanzimasitadesyoh	1. irassyattaroh 1. oidenasattaroh 2. irassyattadesyoh 2 oidenasattadesyoh 2. oideninattadesyoh 2. irassyaimasitadesyoh 2. oidenasaimasitadesyoh 2. oideninarimasitadesyoh 2. oideasobasitadesyoh 3. oideasobasimasitadesyoh
fut. pas. neg	**konandaroh** **konakattaroh**	1. mairimasendesitaroh 1. sanzimasendesitaroh	1. irassyaranakattaroh 2. irassyaranakattadesyoh 2. oidenasaranandadesyoh 2. oideninaranandadesyoh 2. irassyaimasendesitaroh 2. oidenasaimasendesitaroh 2. oideninarimasendesitaroh 2. oideasobasanandaroh 3. oideasobasimasendesitaroh

CONDITIONAL

		Column A	Column B
pres. pos.	**kureba**	1. mairimasureba 1. sanzimasureba	1. irassyareba 1. oidenasareba 1. oideninareba 2. irassyaimasureba 2. oidenasaimasureba 2. oideninarimasureba 2. oideasobaseba 3. oideasobasimasureba
pres. neg.	**konakereba**	1. mairibaseneba 1. sanzimaseneba	1. irassyaraneba 1. oidenasaraneba 1. irassyaimasennara 1. oideninaranakereba 2. oidenasaimasennara 2. oideasobasannara 3. oideasobasimasennara
pas. pos.	**kitara**	1. mairimasitara 1. sanzimasitara	1. irassyattara 1. oidenasattara 1. oideninattara 2. irassyaimasitara 2. oidenasaimasitara 2. oideninarimasitara 2. oideasobasitara 3. oideasobasimasitara
pas. neg.	**konandara** **konakattara**	1. mairimasendesitara 1. sanzimasendesitara	1. irassyaranandara 1. irassyaranakattara 1. oidenasaranandara 1. oidenasaranakattara 2. irassyaimasendesitara 2. oidenasaimasendesitara 2. oideasobasanandara 2. oideasobasanakattara 3. oideasobasimasendesitara

---

JAPANESE VERBS DEFINED IN ENGLISH
Continued from previous page (lower section)

umphant, be elated with victory, be proud of victory.

Katiuru (7a ex) to achieve, earn, win.

Katiwataru (6 en) to wade, ford.

Kaedasu (8 ex) to bail, pump, drain.

Kaerimiru (7 en) to look back, turn; to reflect on, consider.

Kaeru (6 en) to return, come back; to overturn; to hatch.

Kaeru (7 ex) to change, sift,

transform, modify, vary; to substitute, alternate; to exchange, convert, barter.

Kaesu (8 ex) to return, pay back, restore; to overturn, upset; to hatch, breed.

Kagamaru (6 en) to bend, bow, bend, be hunchbacked.

Kagaru (6 ex) to darn.

Kagayakasu (8 ex) to brighten, light up, let shine.

Kagayaku (3 en) to shine, beam,

Continued on next page (lower section)

fut. pos.	koyohnara		1. irassyarohnara
		1. mairimasyohnara	1. oidenasarohnara
		1. sanzimasyohnara	2. irassyaimasyohnara
			2. oidenasaimasyohnara
			2. oideninarimasyohnara
			2. irassyaimasudesyohnara
			2. oideasobasudesyohnara
			3. oideasobasimasudesyohnara
fut. neg.	kumainara		1. irassyarumainara
		1. mairimasumainara	1. oidenasarumainara
		1. sanzimasumainara	2. irassyaimasumainara
			2. oidenasaimasumainara
			2. oidenasaimasendesyohnara
			3. oideasobasimasumainara

IMPERATIVE

pos.	koi		1. irassyai
			1. oidenasai
			2. irassyaimase
			2. oidenasaimase
			2. oideasobase
			3. oideasobasimase
neg.	kuna		1. irassyaruna
	kuruna		1. oidenasaruna
			2. irassyaimasuna
			2. oidenasaimasuna
			2. oideasobasuna
			3. oideasobasimasuna

ADJECTIVAL

pos.	kuru	1. mairimasuru	1. irassyaru
		1. sanzimasuru	1. oidenasaru
			1. oideninaru
			2. oidenasaimasu(ru)
			2. oideninarimasu(ru)
			2. oideasobasu
			3. oideasobasimasu(ru)
neg.	konu	1. mairimasen(u)	1. irassyaran(u, ai)
	konai	1. sanzimasen(u)	1. oidenasaran(u, ai)
			1. oideninaran(u, ai)
			2. irassyaimasen(u)
			2. oidenasaimasen(u)
			2. oideasobasen(u, ai)
			3. oideasobasimasen(u)

CONJUNCTIVE

pos.	kite	1. mairimasite	1. irassyatte
		1. sanzimasite	1. oidenasatte
			1. oideninatte
			2. irassyaimasite
			2. oidenasaimasite
			2. oideninarimasite
			2. oideasobasite
			3. oideasobasimasite
neg.	konaide		1. irassyaranaide
		1. mairimasende	1. oidenasaranaide
		1. sanzimasende	1. oideninaranaide
			2. irassyaimasende
			2. oidenasaimasende
			2. oideasobasanaide
			3. oideasobasimasende

(-naide or -nakutte, alternative)

JAPANESE VERBS DEFINED IN ENGLISH
Continued from previous page (lower section)

brighten, sparkle, glitter, be luminous, be radiant.

Kagerasu (8 ex) to dim, cloud, obscure.

Kageru (6 en) to dim, cloud; to be obscured, be darkened.

Kagiru (6 ex) to limit, restrict, confine.

Kagiru (6 en) to be limited, be peculiar to.

Kagu (2 ex) to lack, fail; to break, chip.

Kagu (2 ex) to smell, scent, sniff.

Continued on next page (lower section)

THE ELEVENTH B CONJUGATION (a)

INDICATIVE

pres. pos.	suru	does
pres. neg.	sen(u)	does not
pas. pos.	sita	did
pas. neg.	senanda	did not
	sinakatta	
fut. pos.	siyoh	will do
fut. neg.	sumai	will not do
fut. pas. pos.	sitaroh	will have done
fut. pas. neg.	senandaroh	will not have done
	sinakattaroh	

CONDITIONAL

pres. pos.	sureba	if does
pres. neg.	seneba	if does not
pas. pos.	sitara	if did
pas. neg.	senandara	if did not
	sinakattara	
fut. pos.	siyohnara(ba)	if would do
fut. neg.	sumainara(ba)	if would not do

IMPERATIVE

pos.	sei	do!
	seyo	
neg.	suna	do not!
	suruna	

ADJECTIVAL

pos.	suru	doing
neg.	senu	not doing

CONJUNCTIVE

pos.	site	does and
neg.	sinaide	does not and

COLLOQUIAL JAPANESE VERBS DEFINED IN ENGLISH
Continued from previous page (lower section)

Kaikaburu (6 ex) to pay too much for; to over-rate, over-estimate.

Kaikomu (4 ex) to rake in, collect; to hold under arms.

Kaisimeru (7 ex) to buy up, forestall.

Kaisuru (11b ex) to understand, comprehend.

Kaisuru (11b en) to meet, assemble; to encounter.

Kaitumamu (4 ex) to sum up, abridge, summarize.

Kaziru (6 ex) to gnaw, nibble.

Kakaeru (7 ex) to hold in arms, embrace.

Kakageru (7 ex) to lift up, hold up, raise, hoist, exhibit.

Kakaru (6 en) to hang, be suspended; to weigh; to depend on; to be caught; to need, require; to concern.

Kakaseru (7 ex) to cause to write, have (a letter) written, have (a picture) painted.

Kakawaru (6 en) to concern, af-

Continued on next page (lower section)

THE ELEVENTH B CONJUGATION (b)

PART I (all persons)		PART II (1st & 3rd persons)	PART III (2nd person)

INDICATIVE

pres. pos.   suru   1. simasu
                 1. itasimasu

1. sinasaru
2. nasaimasu
2. asobasu
3. asobasimasu

pres. neg.   sen(u)   1. simasen
                 1. itasimasen

1. sinasaran
2. nasaimasen
2. asobasan
3. asobasimasen

pas. pos.   sita   1. simasita
             1. itasimasita

1. sinasatta
1. nasatta
2. asobasita
3. asobasimasita

pas. neg.   senanda   1. simasendesita
           sinakatta   1. itasimasendesita

1. nasarananda
1. sinasarananda
2. asobasananda
3. asobasimasendesita

fut. pos.   siyoh   1. simasyoh
             1. itashimasyoh

1. nasaimasyoh
2. sinasarimasyoh
3. asobasimasyoh

fut. neg.   sumai   1. simasumai
             1. itasimasumai

1. nasarumai
1. sinasarumai
2. asobasumai
3. asobasimasumai

fut. pas. pos.   sitaroh   1. simasitaroh
                    1. itasimasitaroh

1. nasattaroh
1. sinasattaroh
2. nasaimasitaroh
2. sinasaimasitaroh
2. asobasitaroh
3. asobasimasitaroh

fut. pas. neg.   senandaroh   1. simasendesitaroh
               sinakattaroh   1. itasimasendesitaroh

1. nasaranandaroh
1. nasaranakattaroh
2. nasaimasendesitaroh
2. sinasaimasendesitaroh
2. asobasanandaroh
3. asobasimasendesitaroh

CONDITIONAL

pres. pos.   sureba   1. simasureba
              1. itasimasureba

1. sinasareba
2. nasaimasureba
2. sinasaimasureba
2. asobaseba
3. asobasimasureba

pres. neg.   seneba   1. simaseneba
             1. itasimaseneba

1. nasaraneba
2. nasaimaseneba
2. sinasaimaseneba
2. asobasaneba
3. asobasimasaneba

JAPANESE VERBS DEFINED IN ENGLISH
Continued from previous page (lower section)

fect; to be concerned in; to adhere to.

Kakeau (10 en) to negotiate with, consult with, bargain with.

Kakedasu (8 en) to run out.

Kakehanareru (7 en) to be far apart, be far off; be at a distance.

Kakekomu (4 en) to run in.

Kakemawaru (6 en) to run about.

Kakenaosu (8 ex) to rehand; to reweight.

Kakeru (6 en) to run, dart, gallop; to soar, fly.

Kakeru (7 ex) to hang, suspend; to weight; to span, to lock; to pour on; to sit down; to cover.

Kakeru (7 en) to lack, be miss-

Continued on next page (lower section)

pas. pos.	sitara	1. simasitara 1. itashimasitara	1. nasattara 1. sinasattara 2. nasaimasitara 2. sinasaimasitara 2. asobasitara 3. asobasimasitara
pas. neg.	senandara sinakattara	1. simasendesitara 1. itasimasendesitara	1. nasaranandara 2. sinasaranandara 2. asobasanandara 3. asobasimasendesitara
fut. pos.	siyohnaraba	1. simasyohnara 1. itasimasyohnara	2. nasaimasyohnara 2. sinasarimasyohnara 3. asobasimasyohnara
fut. neg.	sumainara	1. simasumainara 1. itasimasumainara	2. nasaimasumainara 2. sinasarimasumainara 3. asobasimasumainara

IMPERATIVE

pos.	sei seyo		1. nasai 1. sinasai 2. nasaimase 2. asobase 3. asobasimase
neg.	suna suruna		1. nasaruna 2. nasaimasuna 2. asobasuna 3. asobasimasuna

ADJECTIVAL

pos.	suru	1. simasuru 1. itasimasuru	1. nasaru 2. nasaimasuru 2. asobasu 3. asobasimasuru
neg.	senu	1. simasenu 1. itasimasenu	1. nasaranu 2. nasaimasenu 2. asobasanu 3. asobasimasenu

CONJUNCTIVE

pos.	site	1. simasite 1. itashimasite	1. nasatte 2. nasaimasite 2. asobasite 3. asobasimasite
neg.	sinaide	1. simasende 1. itasimasende	1. nasaranaide 2. nasaimasende 2. asobasanaide 3. asobasimasende

---

JAPANESE VERBS DEFINED IN ENGLISH
Continued from previous page (lower section)

ing; to be broken, chipped; to wane; to bet, wager, risk.

Kakezuru (6 en) to run about, busy oneself about.

Kakiireru (7 ex) to rake in; to write in.

Kakikaeru (7 ex) to rewrite, renew.

Kakikakeru (7 ex) to begin to write.

Kakikesu (8 ex) to scratch out, wipe out.

Kakikomu (4 ex) to carry in, bear into; to rake in, shovel in; to write in, inscribe.

Kakikumoru (6 en) to become cloudy, become overcast.

Kakikureru (7 en) to be blinded.

Kakimawasu (8 ex) to stir up, churn; to disturb; to rummage, ransack.

Kakimazeru (7 ex) to mix by stirring; to mix up.

Kakimidasu (8 ex) to confuse, throw into confusion, disarrange.

Kakimorasu (8 ex) to omit in writing.

Kakimusiru (6 ex) to scratch, tear.

Kakinaosu (8 ex) to rewrite, write afresh.

Kakinarasu (8 ex) to level, rake smooth; to play (musical instruments).

Continued on page 77 (lower section)

Festival at the Heian Shrine

Shinto Temple

As a simple verb there is only one verb **suru** to this conjugation. But this verb being of the nature somewhat like an auxiliary verb of the English, may serve as a suffix, to a noun, adjective or adverb to convert it into a verb.

Among adjectives and adverbs serving for this purpose are so-called onomatopoetic terms, i.e., imitating sounds, originally. For example: gatagatasuru, to be shaky; bikubikusuru, to be scared; seiseisuru, to be soothing.

Nouns converted into verbs by suffixing -suru are called nominal verbs, and are divided into two classes; namely, nominal verbs consisting of a single Chinese character and those consisting of two or more Chinese characters, with Chinese sounds* in either cases.

*REMARKS: The Chinese sound means the sound used in Japan in connection with the characters originally brought from China. Japan learned sounds of Chinese characters from Chinese some 1500 years ago, and handed down and preserved from generation to generation. But of course some of the sounds undoubtedly have undergone marked changes, in the meantime in China, also changes in sounds during so many centuries of time must be great, with the results that today the Chinese and Japanese sounds for the same one character differ widely especially in vowel qualities.

NOMINAL VERBS
Consisting of a Single Chinese Character with Chinese Sound

These characters, when used without a suffix usually serve as nouns denoting action or state, but if the verb of the 11th b conjugation is suffixed, they serve as verbs. Hence they are called nominal verbs—or verbs derived from nouns. Some of the most popularly used verbs belonging to this class are included in the list of the colloquial Japanese verbs. But here nearly all nominal verbs of single Chinese character are listed including those appeared in the popular list. Because of the fact that many nominal verbs of single character take a modified form of suffix and those of two or more characters invariably take the regular suffix -suru, the verbs of single character are here listed separately from those of two or more characters. The modified form of -suru is -zuru or -ziru, usually belonging to the 7th conjugation but is sometimes conjugated in the same way as -suru, substituting z in place of s all way through, but with no other change as far as the rest of the letters is concerned. This modified suffix is limited to verbs with the stem ending in N or H. The verbs an, ben, tin, nen, oh, tuh, hoh, etc. takes -zuru or -ziru always. But men, han, kan, ken, koh, huh, tyoh, etc. take -suru for one sense and -zuru or -ziru for another sense. One other peculiarity of verbs in this class is that if the syllable of the stem ends in tu it is invariably changed into s before the suffix -suru is attached to it. Thus: for example: atu(as-) means the change of the syllable tu into s, making in this case assuru. (z) after the stem indicates -zuru or -ziru. (zu) if zuru is preferable and (zi) if -ziru is preferable.

Ai, ex. to love.
Atu (as-), ex. to press.
An (z), en. to be anxious.
Bai, en. to double.
Baku, ex. to arrest.
Baku, ex. to controvert.
Batu (bas-), ex. to punish.
Ben (z), ex. to distinguish.

Ben (z), en. to controvert.
Boku, ex, to divine.
Boku, ex. to shepherd.
Botu (bos-), en. to sink.
Botu (bos-), en. to die.
Da, ex. en. to spit on.
Dai, en. to entitle.
Daku, en. to consent to.
Dan (z), ex. to speak.
Datu (das-), ex. to take off, escape; to omit.
Di, ex. to cure; en, to heal.
Dyo, ex. to divide.
Ei (z), ex. to compose, sing.
Ei (z), en. to reflect, cast a shadow.
Eki, ex. to benefit.
En (z), ex. to perform.
Etu (es-), en. to have an audience with.
Ga, ex. to celebrate.
Ga, en. to lie down.
Ga, ex. to bridge across.
Geki, en. to be excited.
Gen (z), en. to decrease; ex. to deduct.
Gi, ex. to discuss, debate.
Gi, ex, to imitate, pretend.
Gin (z), ex. to chant, recite.
Guh, ex. to treat.
Gyo, ex. to ride, drive.
Ha, ex. to send out, despatch.
Hai, ex. to repeat, abolish.
Hai, ex. to exclude, expel.
Haku, ex. to gain, win, obtain.
Han, en, to oppose, be in contrary to.
Han (z), ex. to decide, solve, divine.
Hatu (has-), en. to start; ex. to emit, give off.
Hei, ex. to engage, call, hire.
Hen, en. to incline, lean.
Hen, (z), ex. to exchange, alter.
Hi, ex. to keep secret, hide from.
Hin, en. to be on the verge of.
Hin, en. to become poor.
Hoh (z), ex. to dedicate, observe, obey.
Hoh, (z), ex. to report, inform.
Hoh (z), en. to die, pass away.
Hu, ex. to subjoin, append.
Huh, ex. to hint, suggest.
Huku, en. to bend down, stoop.
Huku, en, to obey, submit; ex. to subdue.
Hun, en. to act in the part of.
I, ex. to cure, remedy.
Itu (is-), ex. to let get away, miss, lose.
Ka, en. to change, turn, become.
Ka, ex. to inflect, impose.
Ka, ex. to levy, charge, impose.
Ka, en. to marry (a man).
Kai, en. to meet, assemble.
Kai, ex. to understand, comprehend.

Kan, en. to be connected with.
Kan, ex. & en. to cap, crown.
Kan (z), ex. to feel, be moved, be impressed.
Kei, ex. to respect, honor, revere.
Ken, ex. to inspect, examine.
Ken (z), ex. to present, offer, dedicate.
Ketu (kes-), ex. to decide, resolve, determine.
Ki, ex. to write down, record.
Ki, ex. to expect.
Ki, ex. to attribute to; en. to side with.
Kin (z), ex. to prohibit.
Kitu (kis-), ex. to take, eat, smoke.
Koh (z), ex. to devise.
Kutu (kus-), en. to bend, give away.
Kyoh, ex. to furnish, offer.
Kyoh, (z), en. to enjoy, be amused.
Kyuh, en. to be in want.
Kyuh, ex. to supply, provide.
Mei (z), ex. to command.
Men, en. to face.
Mi, ex. to charm, bewitch.
Nan (z), ex. to condemn, censure.
Nen (z), ex. to pray.
Netu (nes-), ex. & en. to heat.
Nin (z), ex. to nominate, appoint.
Oh (z), en. to comply with, answer.
Oku, en. to fear, be timid.
Rei, en. to command.
Rei, en. to salute, greet, return thanks.
Retu (res-), en. to attend, be present.
Ri, ex. to gain, benefit.
Ritu (ris-), ex. to judge.
Roh, en. to labor, trouble.
Ron (z), ex. to argue, discuss, debate.
Rui, en. to resemble.
Ryaku, ex. to abbreviate.
Ryoh, ex. to finish.
Ryoh, ex. to govern, rule.
Setu (ses-), en. to touch, adjoin, meet.
Setu (ses-), ex. to moderate, economize.
Sen(zu), ex. to think over.
Sen(zi), ex. to boil, decoct.
Sei, ex. to make, manufacture.
Sei, ex. to check, control.
Si, en. to die.
Sii, ex. to murder.
Sin(z), ex. to believe.
Situ (sis-), ex. to lose.
Soh, ex. to effect, report to the Emperor.
Son, en. to lose.
Son(z), to injure, hurt.
Son, en. to exist.
Sui, en. to guess.
Sya, en. to apologize, thank.
Syo, en. to manage, conduct.
Syoh, ex. to call, name, pretend.

67

Syoh(z), ex. to produce, cause; en. to arise, grow.
Syuku, ex. to congratulate, celebrate.
Tai, en, to face, oppose, correspond.
Taku, ex. to trust with, to pretend.
Tatu (tas-), en. to reach.
Tan(z), ex. to deplore, lament.
Tan(z), ex. to play a music instrument.
Tin(z), ex. to state, explain.
Tyaku, en. to arrive.
Tyoh(z), en. to grow, be efficient in.
Tyoh(z), ex. to examine, detect.
Tuh(z), en. to communicate; ex. to let through.
Tyuh, ex. to put to death.
Tei, ex. to offer, give.
Teki, en. to be suitable.
Ten(z), ex. to change, turn.
To, ex. to wager.
Toh(z), ex. to throw.
Wa, ex. to harmonize with.
Yaku, ex. to promise.
Yaku, ex. to translate.
Yoh, ex. to need, require.
Yoku, en. to bathe.
Za, en. to sit down.
Zei, ex. to flourish.
Zyo, ex. to excuse.
Zyuku, en. to ripen.
Zyun(z), en. to model.

The prefix of courteousness is rarely used with these verbs of a single Chinese characters except in a few cases as follows:

go-rannasaru, to see (the courteous form of miru and is limited to the part III of the conjugation).

gyo-sinnaru, to sleep (the courteous form of neru and is limited to the part III of the conjugation).

NOMINAL VERBS
Consisting of two or more Chinese characters
with Chinese sounds

Nominal verbs of two or more Chinese characters take the suffix -suru without any modification. Most of these verbs are the creation during Meiji period (1868-1912), although some are of older origin. In a way, these verbs may be regarded to be a part of the book language, as they are most often see in written Japanese. The more educated and cultured people who naturally read more, make use of these verbs in ordinary conversation than the less educated individuals. People used to be fond of using these verbs as a pretense of culture and education, although today they are more popularly used. In the list here are given the more important nominal verbs of two or more characters. These are not included in the list of the colloquial Japanese verbs.

akusyu, en. to shake hands.
anki, ex. to know by heart, commit to memory.

ansin, en. to feel easy, be at ease.
appaku, ex. to oppress, press, push.
attoh, ex. to overwhelm, overcome, oppress.
baibai, ex. to buy and sell, trade, deal in.
baika, en. to increase two-fold, double.
baikai, ex. to mediate, transmit, be instrumental in.
bakko, en. to dominate, be rampant.
bakudatu, (hakudatu), ex. to deprive of, strip of.
bakuro, en. to be exposed, come to light; ex. to disclose, divulge.
bakuhatu, en. to explode, blow up; ex. to blast, explode.
bakuretu, en. to burst, explode, detonate.
bankai, ex. to regain, recover, revive.
bari, ex. to insult, abuse, rail at.
batoh, ex. to insult, abuse, rail at.
batubyoh, en. to weigh anchor.
bekke, en. to found a branch family.
bekkyo, en. to live separately.
benbetu, ex. to distinguish, discern.
bengo, ex. to plead for, defend.
benkai, en. to vindicate, explain.
benkyoh, ex. to study, be diligent.
bentatu, ex. to chastize, whip.
bessi, ex. to despise, scorn.
bikoh, en. to travel incognito.
binran, ex. to throw into disorder.
bohgai, ex. to disturb, obstruct, bother.
bohgyo, en. to defend, guard against.
bohken, en. to risk, venture.
bohkyaku, ex. to forget.
bokki, en. to rise up, stand up.
bokkoh, en. to rise suddenly.
buiku, ex. to bring up, raise, nurse.
bunkai, ex. en. to analyze, decompose.
bunretu, en. to break up, disintegrate.
bunri, en. to separate, split.
bunritu, en. to separate from.
buzyoku, ex. to abuse, insult, affront.
byohki, en. to be ill, fall sick.
byohsya, ex. to depict, describe, sketch.
dakyoh, en. to confer, negotiate.
daihitu, en. to write for another.
daisyo, en. to write for another.
dansoh, en. to wear male attire.
danwa, en. to talk, converse.
danzetu, en. to become extinct, be severed.
denbun, ex. to hear through others.
dentatu, ex. to transmit, convey.
doryoku, en. to labor, struggle.
dokusatu, ex. to kill with poison.
dyuh-huku, (tyoh-huku), en. to be repeated, double.
dyuhkyo, en, to reside, live at.
eiten, en. to be promoted.
ekken, en. to be received in audience.
enryo, en. to be reserved, hesitate.
gaitoh, en. to correspond, come under.
ganzoh, ex. to forge, counterfeit.

geisai, en. to marry, wed. (said of a man)
geizi, ex. to glare, stare.
gekitai, ex. to repulse, dislodge.
giketu, ex. to decide on, vote for.
gisoh, ex. to equip (a ship).
gisyoh, en. to perjure, give false testimony.
gizoh, ex. to forge, counterfeit.
gohdatu, ex. to rob, extort.
gohkan, ex. to assault, attack.
gohmon, ex. to torture.
gubi, ex. to possess, be furnished with.
gyakushyuh, en. to counter-attack.
gyakutai, ex. to ill-treat.
gyohten, en. to be consternated.
haiboku, en. to be defeated, be repulsed.
haietu, en. to be received in audience.
haihu, ex. to distribute.
haikai, en. to wander about.
haiseki, ex. to reject, exclude.
haisetu, ex. to discharge.
haisi, ex. to abolish.
hakai, ex. to destroy, demolish.
haken, ex. to send, despatch.
hakkan, en. to sweat, perspirate.
hakkan, ex. to publish.
hakken, ex. to find, discover.
hakkoh, ex. to publish, edit.
hakkoh, en. to ferment.
hamon, ex. to excommunicate.
hanbai, ex. to sell.
handan, ex. to judge, decide, interpret.
hanketu, ex. to judge.
hanmo, en. to grow luxuriantly.
hanpu, ex. to distribute.
hanpuku, ex. to repeat.
hansyoku, en. to breed, multiply.
hantai, en. to oppose, object.
haretu, en. to burst, explode.
heikoh, en. to be defeated, be beaten.
heiritu, en. to stand side by side.
hekieki, en. to shrink back, give in.
henkyaku, ex. to return, repay.
henkoh, ex. to change, alter.
henpoh, en. to retaliate, return.
henreki, en. to wander about, travel around.
hensan, ex. to edit, compile.
hensin, en. to change mind.
hensyu, ex. to defraud, swindle.
hensyuh, ex. to edit.
hiboh, ex. to slander, abuse.
hige, en. to humble oneself.
higi, ex. to criticize, censure.
higo, ex. to protect, cover.
hikaku, ex. to compare.
hikan, en. to be pessimistic.
hikki, ex. to write down.

hikoh, en. to fly, aviate.
hinseki, ex. to reject, despise.
hiroh, ex. to announce.
hiroh, en. to be tired, be fatigued.
hitei, ex. to deny.
hitteki, en. to be a match.
hittyuh, ex. to castigate with a pen.
hitudan, en. to converse with pen.
hizoh, ex. to prize, treasure.
hoiku, ex. to bring up, nurse.
hohdoh, ex. to report, inform.
hohkoh, en. to enter service.
hohkoku, ex. to report.
hohmon, ex. to visit, call.
hohnin, en. to leave alone.
hohsoh, ex. to broadcast.
hohzyo, ex. to assist, protect.
hokoh, en. to walk.
hosa, ex. to assist, help.
hosyoh, ex. to secure, guarantee.
hukoku, ex. to decree, proclaim.
hukumei, en. to report results of a mission.
hukusyuh, en. to retaliate.
hukuyoh, en. to keep in mind.
hukyuh, en. to spread, diffuse.
hunbetu, en. to judge, discern, consider.
hungai, en. to be indignant.
hunin, en. to start for one's post.
hunka, en. to erupt.
hunki, en. to rouse up.
hunpatu, en. to make an effort.
hunsitu, ex. and en. to lose, to get lost.
hunsyutu, en. to gush, out, erupt.
huntoh, en. to struggle, labor hard.
hutyaku, en. to adhere, stick.
huyoh, ex. to nurse, feed.
huzyo, ex. to assist, aid.
hyohgi, ex. to discuss, confer.
hyohron, ex. to review, criticize.
igon, (yuigon), en. to leave a will.
ihan, en. to violate.
ikketu, en. to come to a decision.
imon, ex. to console, condole with.
inin, ex. to give in charge, authorize.
insyoku, en. to eat and drink.
insyu, en. to drink wine.
inton, en. to retire from the world.
irai, ex. to request, trust, depend on.
issoh, ex. to make a clean sweep.
itaku, ex. to consign, intrust.
iten, en. to move, change abode.
itiran, ex. to take a look.
itti, en. to agree, accord.
kaidan, en. to converse, have an interview.
kaigoh, en. to meet, have a meeting.
kaihuku, en. and ex. to recover, restore.

71

kaiketu, ex. to settle, solve, decide.
kaiko, ex. to discharge, dismiss.
kaisya, en. to be well known, be familiar.
kakketu, en. to spit blood.
kakugo, en. to apprehend, anticipate, be ready.
kakuri, ex. to isolate, segregate.
kakusaku, ex. to plan, scheme, project.
kakutei, ex. to fix, decide.
kakutoku, ex. to acquire, obtain.
kakutyoh, ex. to expand, enlarge.
kanbetu, ex. to distinguish, differentiate.
kandoh, ex. to disinherit.
kangai, ex. to irrigate.
kanka, ex. to influence, convert.
kankoku, ex. to advise, counsel.
kansi, ex. to watch, observe.
kansoh, ex. and en. to dry, desiccate.
kansyoh, en. to interfere, meddle with.
kantei, ex. to appraise, judge.
kanzyoh, ex. to count, calculate.
kassoh, en. to glide, slide.
katudoh, en. to be active.
katuyaku, en. to take active part.
keibetu, ex. to scorn, disdain, slight.
keibo, ex. to esteem, adhere.
keihatu, ex. to enlighten, develop, educate.
keiken, ex. to experience, undergo.
keikoku, ex. to give warning.
keirei, en. to bow, salute, make obeissance.
keiryuh, ex. to moor.
keisai, ex. to publish, insert.
keisan, ex. to count, calculate.
keisi, ex. to disregard, slight.
keisya, en. to incline, slant.
keitai, ex. to carry, bring.
keiyaku, ex. to promise, contract, agree.
keiyoh, en. to express figuratively.
keizyoh, ex. to add up, sum up.
kekkin, en. to be absent from duty.
kenbun, ex. to inspect.
kenbutu, ex. to visit, do sight-seeking.
kenka, en. to fight, quarrel.
kenkyuh, ex. to study, research.
kensa, ex. to inspect, examine.
kenma, ex. to polish, cultivate, refine.
kennin, ex. to hold an additional post.
kensan, ex. to study.
kensetu, ex. to build, construct.
kensei, ex. to check, restrain.
kensi, en. to hold an inquest.
kenson, en. to be modest.
kentei, ex. to examine, certify, standardize.
kentiku, ex. to build, construct.
kenyaku, en. to economize.
kesoh, en. to fall in love.
kesseki, en. to be absent.

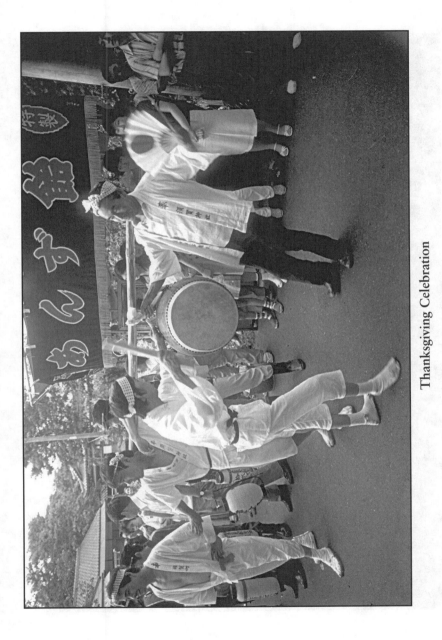

Thanksgiving Celebration

Local Restaurant

kettei, ex. to determine, decide, resolve.
kettoh, en. to fight a duel.
ketubetu, en. to bid farewell.
ketugi, ex. to decide, resolve.
kiboh, ex. to wish, hope, expect.
kiin, en. to be attributable to.
kikoku, en. to return to home country.
kinen, ex. to commemorate.
kin-en, en. to abstain from smoking.
kinko, ex. to confine, imprison.
kinsi, ex. to prohibit.
kinsyu, en. to abstain from liquor.
kintyoh, en. to strain.
kioku, ex. to remember, recall.
kiroku, ex. to record, note.
kison, ex. to injure, destroy.
kityaku, en. to come back, arrive at.
kityoh, en. to come back to home land.
kodi, ex. to persist in.
kogi, en. to doubt, hesitate.
kohdei, en. to adhere to, cling to.
kohgeki, ex. to attack.
kohgi, en. to protect, object.
kohgun, en. to march.
kohkoh, en. to be an obedient son.
kohsaku, ex. to till, cultivate.
kohsan, en. to surrender.
kohsoku, ex. to bind, restrain.
kozi, ex. to refuse, decline.
kubetu, ex. to distinguish.
kubun, ex. to divide, distribute.
kugaku, en. to study under adverse condition.
kuhuh, ex. to devise, contrive.
kumen, ex. to manage, devise.
kumon, en. to be in agony, struggle.
kunrei, en. to instruct, direct.
kunzi, en. to instruct.
kuroh, en. to worry, suffer.
kusin, en. to labor, suffer.
kuttaku, en. to be vexed.
kyohdoh, en. to join, cooperate.
kyohgi, ex. to confer with.
kyoh-iku, ex. to educate, instruct.
kyohkatu, ex. to threaten, intimidate.
kyohki, en. to become mad.
kyohkyuh, ex. to supply, furnish.
kyohran, en. to be driven mad.
kyohryoku, en. to cooperate.
kyohsoh, en. to run a race.
kyohsoh, en. to complete.
kyohzyu, ex. to teach, instruct.
kyoka, ex. to permit.
kyokuhitu, en. to pervert in writing.
kyozetu, to reject, refuse.
kyuhdai, en. to be promoted, pass examination.
kyuhgoh, ex. to call together, convoke.

kyuhkei, en. to rest.
kyuhkoh, en. to go in a hurry.
kyuhsi, en. to pause, stop.
kyuhsoku, en. to rest, relax, repose.
kyuh-yoh, en. to rest, relax, recuperate.
man-en, en. to spread, extend.
manzoku, en. to be satisfied, be contented.
masatu, ex. to rub, chafe.
maisoh, ex. to inter, bury.
massatu, ex. to erase, efface, cancel.
meimei, ex. to name, christen.
meimoku, en. to close the eyes, die.
meitei, en. to get intoxicated.
meiwaku, en. to be annoyed, be embarrassed.
mendan, en. to talk with, interview.
menkai, en. to meet, see, interview.
menzyo, ex. to exempt, release.
mitubai, ex. to sell secretly, smuggle.
miituyunyuh, ex. to smuggle.
mondoh, en. to catechise.
monzetu, en. to die of agony.
musoh, en. to dream, be in a reverie.
muzyun, en. to be self-contradictory.
nangi, en. to suffer hardship.
nanka, en. to soften, yield.
nenshoh, en. to burn, inflame.
netuzoh, ex. to fabricate, fake.
nikuziki, en. to eat flesh.
ninsiki, ex. to recognize.
ninsin, en. to conceive, be pregnant.
nintai, en. to be patient.
nissan, en. to pay daily visit.
noh-hu, ex. to pay, supply.
nyuhkoku, en. to enter the country.
nyuhrai, en. to enter, come in.
nyuhsen, en. to be selected.
ohda, ex. to hit, strike, assault.
oh-en, ex. to aid, assist, support.
ohto, ex. to vomit.
okudan, ex. to conjecture.
okusoku, ex. to guess, suppose.
raidoh, en. to follow another blindly.
rakkan, en. to be optimistic.
reihai, ex. to worship.
reiraku, en. to go to ruin.
reisyoh, ex. to sneer, jeer at, ridicule.
rekisatu, ex. to kill by running over.
rekisi, en. to get killed by running over.
rengoh, en. to combined with, join.
renma, ex. to train, temper.
renzoku, en. to continue, be connected.
rien, ex. to divorce.
rikai, ex. to understand, comprehend.
rikan, en. to estrange, alienate.
rippuku, en. to be angry.
rituron, en. to argue.

rohdoh, en. to labor, work.
rohdoku, ex. to read aloud, recite.
ryohdi, ex. to treat, cure.
ryohkai, ex. to understand.
ryohri, ex. to cook.
ryokoh, en. to travel.
saiban, ex. to judge.
saihatu, en. to recur, relapse.
saiku, ex. to work, make shift.
saikutu, ex. to dig out, mine.
saisyuh, ex. to gather, collect.
saiyoh, ex. to adopt, take up.
sakuzyo, ex. to cancel, strike out.
sandan, ex. to contrive, manage.
sankei, en. to visit a temple.
sanpo, en. to take a walk.
sansei, en. to agree with.
sanzyo, ex. to support, help.
sanzyoh, en. to visit.
seien, en. to encourage.
seikatu, en. to live, support oneself.
seikoh, en. to succeed.
seikyuh, ex. to demand, require.
seimei, ex. to declare, announce.
seiri, ex. to adjust.
seiritu, en. to form, consist of.
seisei, ex. to purify, refine.
seisoh, en. to be in full dress.
seisoku, en. to live, exist.
seiton, en. to be arranged, be adjusted.
seiyaku, ex. to pledge, promise.
seizoh, ex. to manufacture.
seizon, en. to exist, live, survive.
sekkei, ex. to plan, scheme.
sengen, en. to declare, proclaim.
senkoku, en. to sentence.
senpuku, en. to lie hidden, lurk.
senryoh, ex. to occupy.
setudan, ex. to cut off, sever.
setumei, ex. to explain.
setuyaku, ex. to economize, save.
sian, ex. to think, consider.
sidoh, ex. to guide, lead.
siboh, en. to die.
sieki, ex. to employ, put to work.
siken, ex. to examine.
sikkoh, ex. to perform, execute.
sinboh, en. to endure, bear, be patient.
sinkoh, en. to believe in.
sinpo, en. to progress.
sinrai, en. to depend upon, rely on.
sinsa, ex. to examine.
singin, en. to groan.
situboh, en. to despair, be disappointed.
situmon, en. to question, inquire.
siyoh, ex. to use, employ.

sohritu, ex. to establish, organize, form.
sohron, en. to dispute, quarrel.
sohsaku, ex. to search for, hunt for.
sohzoh, en. to imagine, suppose.
sosi, ex. to prevent, check.
sokuryoh, ex. to survey.
sonkei, ex. to venerate, respect, honor.
sonzai, en. to exist.
sottoh, en. to swoon, faint.
sotugyoh, en. to graduate.
suh-hai, ex. to venerate, worship.
suisoku, en. to guess, conjecture.
suizyaku, en. to be debilitated.
syakkin, en. to borrow money.
syazai, en. to apologize.
syohdai, ex. to invite.
syohnin, ex. to recognize, acknowledge.
syohsin, en. to be promoted.
syohti, ex. and en. to consent, agree, know, understand.
syohbu, en. to fight, contest.
syohdoku, ex. to disinfect.
syohkai, ex. and en. to introduce, communicate.
syohmei, ex. to prove, certify.
syohrei, ex. to encourage.
syuhgyoh, ex. to study.
syuhsyohrohbai, en. to be alarmed and confused.
syuh-wai, en. to receive a bribe.
taiguh, ex. to treat, receive.
taisyoh, ex. to compare, collate.
takuetu, en. to excel, surpass.
tanren, ex. to train, drill, temper, forge.
tansoku, en. to sigh, lament.
teikoh, en. to resist.
teikei, en. to act in concert.
teisatu, en. to reconnoiter, scout.
teisei, ex. to revise, correct.
teitai, en. to stop, stagnate.
tekisyutu, ex. to quote, extract.
tentaku, en. to move, remove.
tettei, en. to be thorough.
tien, en. to delay, postpone.
tikoku, en. to be late, delay.
tinzyutu, ex. to state, declare.
tiryoh, ex. to treat, cure.
toh-hyoh, ex. to vote.
tohki, en. to rise, advance.
tohroku, ex. to register.
tohryuh, en. to stay, sojourn.
tohtyaku, en. to arrive.
tokusoku, en. to urge, press.
tokusyo, en. to read.
tuhkoh, en. to pass through.
tuhsin, ex. to communicate, correspond.
tyohkoku, ex. to engrave.
tyohsa, ex. to investigate.
tyohsen, en. to challenge.

tyotiku, ex. to save, store.
tyozyutu, en. to write a book.
tyuhkai, ex. to mediate.
tyuhsai, ex. to arbitrate, mediate.
undoh, en. to move, walk, exercise.
unpan, ex. to carry, convey.
unten, ex. to operate, run.
wakai, en. to make up, be reconciled.
wankyoku, en. to be bent, be crooked.
yakkaisi, ex. to feel burdensome.
yakusoku, ex. to promise.
yogen, ex. to prophesy.
yokoku, ex. to predict.
yoti, ex. to foresee.
yudan, en. to be off one's guard.
yuh-ho, en. to take a walk.
yuhryo, en. to worry, apprehend.
yuh-yo, ex. to grant delay, give time.
zaigaku, en. to be in school, be studying.
zairyuh, en. to sojourn, be resident in.
zaitaku, en. to be at home.
zakkyo, en. to reside together.
zange, ex. to confess.
zattoh, en. to crowd together, be congested.
zekkoh, en. to break off friendship.
zenti, ex. to foresee.
zengo, en. to be misplaced.
zenin, ex. to approve, endorse.
zenkai, en. to recover completely.
zensin, en. to progress, proceed.
zikken, ex. to experience, experiment.
zikkoh, ex. to carry out, practice.
zitugen, en. to realize, materialize.
zohka, en. to increase.
zoh-o, ex. to hate, detest.
zyama, en. to hinder, disturb, intrude.
zyasui, ex. to suspect, mistrust.
zyoh-ho, en. to concede, give way.
zyohzyu, ex. to succeed, achieve.
zyohsen, en. to board a ship.
zyohsya, en. to board a car.
zyukkoh, en. to consider carefully.
zyunkai, en. to patrol.
zyunkan, en. to circulate.
zyuhman, en. to be filled.

JAPANESE VERBS DEFINED IN ENGLISH
Continued from page 64 (lower section)

Kakinokeru (7 ex) to rake aside.

Kakinokosu (8 ex) to leave in writing.

Kakiokuru (6 ex) to write to, send a letter to.

Kakiowaru (6 ex) to finish writing.

Kakisagasu (8 ex) to rummage, ransack, scratch for.

Kakisaku (3 ex) to tear, scratch.

Kakisirusu (8 ex) to write down.

Kakisoeru (7 ex) to add in writing, write a postscript to a letter.

Kakisokonau (10 ex) to make a mistake in writing.

Kakisugiru (7 ex) to over-write,

Continued on next page (lower section)

THE ELEVENTH C CONJUGATION (a)

INDICATIVE

pres. pos.	Inuru	goes
pres. neg.	inan(u)	goes not
pas. pos.	inda	did go
pas. neg.	inananda	did not go
	inanakatta	
fut. pos.	inoh	will go
fut. neg.	inumai	will not go
fut. pas. pos.	indaroh	will have gone
fut. pas. neg.	inanandaroh	will not have gone
	inanakattaroh	

CONDITIONAL

pres. pos.	inureba	if goes
pres. neg.	inaneba	if does not go
pas. pos.	indara	if did go
pas. neg.	inanandara	if did not go
fut. pos.	inanakattara	if would go
fut. neg.	inohnara(ba)	if would not go
	inumainara(ba)	

IMPERATIVE

pos.	inei	go!
neg.	inuruna	don't go!

ADJECTIVAL

pos.	inuru	going
neg.	inanu	not going

CONJUNCTIVE

pos.	inde	goes and
neg.	inanaide	goes not and

JAPANESE VERBS DEFINED IN ENGLISH
Continued from previous section (lower section)

write too much.

Kakisugosu (8 ex) same as ka-kisugiru.

Kakitateru (7 ex) to write up; to stir up, beat, churn.

Kakitomeru (7 ex) to make a note of, write down.

Kakiwakeru (7 ex) to make one's way through.

Kakiyoseru (7 ex) to rake together.

Kakomu (4 ex) to enclose in, surround, encircle; to besiege.

Kakotu (9 en) to complain, grumble.

Kakotukeru (7 en) to pretend,

make an excuse.

Kakou (10 ex) to enclose, fence in; to preserve, store, keep.

Kaku (3 ex) to write, draw, paint; to describe; to scratch, claw, scrape.

Kakumau (10 ex) to shelter, screen, harbor; shield, conceal.

Kakureru (7 en) to hide, conceal oneself, lurk; to die.

Kakusu (8 ex) to hide, conceal; to keep secret, screen.

Kamaeru (7 ex) to build, construct; to put oneself in posture, make ready; to feign, pretend.

Kamau (10 ex) to mind, heed,

Continued on next page (lower section)

THE ELEVENTH C CONJUGATION (b)

PART I (all persons)	PART II (1st & 3rd persons)	PART III (2nd person)

INDICATIVE

	PART I	PART II	PART III
pres. pos.	inuru	1. inimasu 1. kaerimasu	1. okaerinasaru 1. okaerininaru 2. okaerinasaimasu 2. okaeriasobasu 3. okaeriasobasimasu
pres. neg.	inan(u)	1. inimasen 1. kaerimasen	1. okaerinasaran 1. okaerininaran 2. okaerinasaimasen 2. okaeriasobasan 3. okaeriasobasimasen
pas. pos.	inda	1. inimasita 1. kaerimasita	1. okaerinasatta 1. okaerininatta 2. okaerinasaimasita 2. okaeriasobasita 3. okaeriasobasimasita
pas. neg.	inananda inanakatta	1. inimasendesita 1. kaerimasendesita	1. okaerinasarananda 1. okaerininarananda 2. okaerinasaimasendesita 2. okaeriasobasananda 3. okaeriasobasimasendesita
fut. pos.	inoh	1. inimasyoh 1. kaerimasyoh	1. okaerinasaroh 1. okaerininaroh 2. okaerinasaimasyoh 2. okaerininarimasyoh 2. okaeriasobasoh 3. okaeriasobasimasyoh
fut. neg.	inumai	1. inimasumai 1. kaerimasumai	1. okaerinasarumai 1. okaerininarumai 2. okaerinasaimasumai 2. okaeriasobasumai 3. okaeriasobasimasumai
fut. pas. pos.	indaroh	1. inimasitaroh 1. kaerimasitaroh	1. okaerinasattaroh 1. okaerininattaroh 2. okaerinasaimasitaroh 2. okaeriasobasitaroh 3. okaeriasobasimasitaroh
fut. pas. neg.	inanandaroh inanakattaroh	1. inanakattadesyoh 1. kaeranakattadesyoh 2. inimasendesitaroh	1. okaerinasaranandaroh 1. okaerinasaranakattaroh 2. okaerinasaimasendesitaroh 2. okaeriasobasanandaroh 3. okaeriasobasimasendesitade- syoh

---

JAPANESE VERBS DEFINED IN ENGLISH
Continued from previous page (lower section)

care; to interfere; to tease, annoy.

Kamikiru (6 ex) to bite off, cut with teeth, chew off.

Kamikorosu (8 ex) to bite to death.

Kamikudaku (3 ex) to crush with teeth, masticate.

Kamisimeru (7 ex) to bite hard, grip with one's teeth; to chew and taste.

Kamituku (3 ex) to bite, snap.

Kamosu (8 ex) to brew; to give rise to, engender, breed.

Kamu (4 ex) to bite, nip, chew, masticate.

Kanaeru (7 ex) to grant, answer; to harmonize, accord.

Kanasimu (4 en) to grieve; to deplore, mourn, lament; to regret.

Kanau (10 en) to agree with, comply with; to respond, correspond; to be granted, be fulfilled; to match, equal to; to be in one's power.

Kanbasiru (6 en) to be shrill, be sharp (in tone).

Kaneru (7 ex) to combine; to be used for two or more purposes.

Kangaeru (7 ex) to think, consider, meditate; to mean, intend.

Continued on next page (lower section)

pres. pos.	inureba	1. inimasureba 1. kaerimasureba	1. okaerinasareba 1. okaerininareba 2. okaerinasaimasureba 2. okaeriasobaseba 3. okaeriasobasimasureba
pres. neg.	inaneba	1. inimasenkereba 1. kaerimasenkereba	1. okaerinasaraneba 1. okaerininaraneba 2. okaerinasaimaseneba 2. okaeriasobasaneba 3. okaeriasobasimaseneba
pas. pos.	indara	1. inimasitara 1. kaerimasitara	1. okaerinasattara 1. okaerininattara 2. okaerinasaimasitara 2. okaeriasobasitara 3. okaeriasobasimasitara
pas. neg.	inanandara	1. inimasendesitara 1. kaerimasendesitara	1. okaerinasaranandara 1. okaerininaranandara 2. okaerinasaimasendesitara 2. okaeriasobasanandara 3. okaeriasobasimasendesitara
fut. pos.	inohnara	1. inimasyohnara 1. kaerimasyohnara	1. okaerinasarohnara 1. okaerininarohnara 2. okaerinasaimasyohnara 2. okaeriasobasohnara 3. okaeriasobasimasyohnara
fut. neg.	inumainara	1. inimasumainara 1. kaerimasumainara	1. okaerinasarumainara 1. okaerininarumainara 2. okaerinasaimasumainara 2. okaeriasobasumainara 3. okaeriasobasimasumainara

JAPANESE VERBS DEFINED IN ENGLISH

Continued from previous page (lower section)

Kangaetuku (3 ex) to recollect, recall.

Kansuru (11b en) to be connected with, concern, have relation to.

Kanzuru (7a or 11b en) to feel; to be impressed with, be affected by.

Karageru (7 ex) to tuck up.

Karamaru (6 en) to twine around, get twisted around.

Karameru (7 ex) to bind; to arrest.

Karamu (4 en) to twine around; to get entangled.

Karareru (7 en) to be carried away; to be impelled, be prompted.

Karasu (8 ex) to let wither; to season; to dry up, exhaust, drain.

Kareru (7 en) to wither, die, perish; to mature, season; to be exhausted, dry up; to get hoarse.

Kariru (7 en) to borrow, lease, rent, hire.

Karitoru (6 ex) to cut down, mow.

Karonzuru (11b ex) to make light of, slight.

Karu (6 ex) to cut. mow, shear, trim; to drive; to hunt, chase; to borrow (same as **Kariru**).

Kasabaru (6 en) to bulk, take up space.

Kasamu (4 en) to grow bulky, swell.

Kasanaru (6 en) to overlap, be piled up; to accumulate.

Kasaneru (7 ex) to pile on, lap; to accumulate; to repeat.

Kasegu (2 ex) to labor, work, earn.

Kasigeru (7 ex) to overbalance, tilt.

Kasigu (2 ex) to cook, boil; to list, incline.

Kasikomaru (6 en) to reverence, revere, obey and respect; to sit straight; to understand; to agree to, assent to.

Kasizuku (3 en) to wait upon, attend on, nurse.

Kasu (8 ex) to lend, loan, lease, rent.

Kasumeru (7 ex) to steal, rob, plunder, pillage.

Kasumu (4 en) to mist, be hazy;

Continued on next page (lower section)

Geisha

Playing the Five-String Biwa

IMPERATIVE

pos.	inei	....	1. okaerinasai
			2. okaerinasaimase
			2. okaeriasobase
			3. okaeriasobasimase
neg.	inuruna	....	1. okaerinasaruna
			2. okaerinasaimasuna
			2. okaeriasobasuna
			3. okaeriasobasimasuna

ADJECTIVAL

pos.	inuru	1. inimasuru	1. okaerinasaru
		1. kaerimasuru	1. okaerininaru
			2. okaerinasaimasuru
			2. okaeriasobasu
			3. okaeriasobasimasuru
neg.	inanu	1. inimasen	1. okaerinasaran
		1. kaerimasen	1. okaerininaran
			2. okaerinasaimasen
			2. okaeriasobasan
			3. okaeriasobasimasen

CONJUNCTIVE

pos.	inde	1. inimasite	1. okaerinasatte
		1. kaerimasite	1. okaerininatte
			2. okaerinasaimasite
			2. okaeriasobasite
			3. okaeriasobasimasite
neg.	inanaide	1. inimasende	1. okaerinasaranaide
		1. kaerimasende	1. okaerinasaranakutte
			2. okaerinasaimasende
			2. okaeriasobasanakutte
			3. okaeriasobasimasende

JAPANESE VERBS DEFINED IN ENGLISH
Continued from previous page (lower section)

to cloud, dim, blur.

Kasuru (6 ex) to graze, shave, skim, brush, scrape.

Kasuru (11b en) to turn into, change into, transform into; to levy tax; to marry.

Katadoru (6 en) to model, fashion.

Katadukeru (7 ex) to put in order, tidy up; to put away; to settle; to put out of the way; to finish.

Kataduku (3 en) to be put in order, be finished; to marry.

Katageru (7 ex) to shoulder, carry on shoulder; to incline, lean.

Katamaru (6 en) to harden, solidify, stiffen, set, consolidate; to congeal, freeze; to gather, assemble; to mass, lump.

Katameru (7 ex) to harden, solidify; to tighten; to congeal, coagulate; to confirm; to fortify, defend, guard.

Katamukeru (7 ex) to incline, lean, slant, tilt, bank; to drink, drain.

Katamuku (3 en) to incline, lean, list; to trend, tend, be disposed; to decline.

Katarau (10 en) to talk together; to engage, promise; to consult.

Katariau (10 en) to talk together, converse with.

Kataru (6 en) to speak, talk, tell, relate, narrate; to recite, chant.

Katayoru (6 en) to step aside; to be out of center; to lean, incline, trend; to be biased, be partial.

Katazikenohsuru (11b en) to be favored with.

Kateru (7 ex) to add.

Katueru (7 en) to be hungry, starve, be starved.

Katugu (2 ex) to carry, shoulder, bear; to deceive, hoax.

Katugu (2 en) to be superstitious.

Kau (10 ez) to buy, purchase, procure; to incur, provoke; to prop up.

Continued on next page (lower section)

The eleventh conjugations A, B, and C are irregular in that the stem vowel is variable in the primary conjugation, and some other verbs are substituted in the polite conjugation.

Conjugation	the verb	stem vowels	verbs used in polite form
11 A	kuru	u o i	mairu sanjiru irassyaru* oidenasaru
11 B	suru	u e i	itasu nasaru sinasaru asobasu
11 C	inuru	u a o	kaeru

These verbs, namely, **kuru, suru** and **inuru** are the only verbs of the 11th conjugation, except **sinuru,** derived from **sinu** (5 en) also conjugated as **inuru.** But they are important through their frequent occurence in ordinary conversations. Moreover, **-suru** is used as a suffix with nominal verbs consisting of two Chinese characters. Some nominal verbs made of a single Chinese character may take **-zuru** or **-ziru** instead of **-suru** (see page 38 and 42). All verbs in **-zuru** or **-ziru** and their derivatives (page 38) are conjugated as in the 7th conjugation.

* The polite form of verbs **oru** (6 en) to live, and **yuku** (3 en) to go is also **lrassyaru.** When **lrassyaru** with its various endings is used in colloquial speech, one should understand which of the three meanings namely, to come, to go, or to live is meant only through the context.

JAPANESE VERBS DEFINED IN ENGLISH
Continued from previous page (lower section)

Kawakasu (8 ex) to dry, desiccate; to drain off.

Kawaku (3 en) to dry up, drain off; to be thirsty, be dry.

Kawariau (10 en) to take turns, alternate with.

Kawaru (6 en) to replace, supercede, be substituted for; to change, alter, vary; to differ, be different; to remove.

Kawasu (8 ex) to exchange; to dodge, avoid.

Kayou (10 en) to go back and forth; to attend, go to; to frequent; to go in and out; to communicate with.

Kazaru (6 ex) to decorate, adorn, ornament, garnish, dress; to trim, beautify, glorify.

Kazasu (8 ex) to shade with hand; to hold up with the hand.

Kazoeru (7 ex) to count, reckon, calculate, compute.

Keburu (6 en) same as **kemuru.**

Kegareru (7 en) to be soiled, defiled, be polluted.

Kegasu (8 ex) to soil, stain, contaminate, pollute; to disgrace, corrupt, defile, profane.

Kemisuru (11b ex) to examine, inspect, review; to read, look for.

Kemuru (6 en) to smoke, smoulder.

Kenasu (8 ex) to belittle, abuse, cry down, disparage.

Kenzuru (7a or 11b ex) to present, offer, dedicate.

Keotosu (8 ex) to kick down.

Keru (6 ex) to kick; to spurn.

Kessuru (11b ex) to decide, determine, fix; to judge.

Kesu (8 ex) to extinguish, put

82

out; to erase, cancel.

Keduru (6 ex) to shave, plane, sharpen, pare, cut; to strike out, erase, confiscate; to cut down, curtail.

Kibamu (4 en) to be tinged with yellow.

Kidoru (6 en) to put on airs, affect, assume.

Kieru (7 en) to go out, die, burn, out, be blown out; to melt away, thaw, disappear; to be worn out, vanish.

Kigatuku (3 en) to recover one's senses, come to; to notice, become aware of; to be attentive.

Kikaeru (7 en) to change one's clothes.

Kikasu (8 en) to tell, explain, inform; to persuade; to exert, sway.

Kikazaru (6 en) to dress up, put on fine clothes.

Kikidasu (8 ex) to find out, hear.

Kikiireru (7 ex) to grant, listen to, assent to, comply with, accede to.

Kikikomu (4 ex) to come to one's ears, come to one's knowledge, be informed of.

Kikimorasu (8 ex) to miss hearing, fail to hear.

Kikinagasu (8 ex) to pay no attention after hearing, pass over after being informed.

Kikinaosu (8 ex) to ask again.

Kikinareru (7 en) to be accustomed to hear, be used to hear.

Kikinokosu (8 ex) to leave unheard.

Kikiotosu (8 ex) to miss hearing.

Kikioyobu (1 ex) to hear, be informed of, get wind of.

Kikitadasu (8 ex) to inquire, ascertain.

Kikitagaru (6 en) to be inquisitive, be curious to hear.

Kikitodokeru (7 ex) to grant, accede to, hear.

Kikitogameru (7 ex) to reprove, find fault with.

Kikitoreru (7 en) to be enchanted with, be enraptured by; to be

capable of being heard, be discernible.

Kikitoru (6 ex) to hear; to catch.

Kikitukeru (7 ex) to hear, overhear; to get wind of; to be used to hear.

Kikiwakeru (7 ex) to understand; to listen to reason.

Kikoeru (7 en) to be able to hear; to be audible; to sound.

Kikosimesu (8 ex ct. exp.) to hear, learn.

Kiku (3 ex) to hear, hear of, learn, be informed; to listen, hearken; to grant, accede to, obey; to ask, inquire, question; to be efficaceous, be effective.

Kimaru (6 en) to be decided, settled, arrive at agreement, come to conclusion, be fixed.

Kimeru (7 ex) to decide, settle, fix, arrange, choose; to resolve, determine.

Kimetukeru (7 ex) to scold.

Kinikakaru (6 en) to weigh upon one's mind.

Kinikakeru (7 ex) to mind; to take to heart.

Kinisuru (11b ex) to take to heart.

Kinitomeru (7 ex) to mind, keep in mind.

Kinzuru (7a or 11b ex) to prohibit, interdict, forbid, ban.

Kiotukeru (7 en) to take care, look after; to mind, be attentive; to look out.

Kirameku (3 en) to glare, glitter, flash.

Kirasu (8 ex) to run out of, run short of.

Kirau (10 ex) to hate, dislike, loathe, detest.

Kireru (7 en) to be cut; to be sharp; to snap apart; to run out of stock.

Kirihanasu (8 ex) to cut off; to separate, sever, divide.

Kirikorosu (8 ex) to slay, slaughter.

Kirimawasu (8 ex) to cut in places; to manage matters skilfully; to carry matters with high hand.

Kirinukeru (7 en) to cut one's way through; to find one's way out.

Kirinuku (3 ex) to cut out, clip out.

Kiriotsu (8 ex) to cut off, chop off.

Kiritaosu (8 ex) to cut down, chop down.

Kiritumeru (7 ex) to shorten, curtail.

Kiriyaburu (6 ex) to cut through.

Kiru (6 ex) to cut, chop, slash; to cut off, disconnect, sever.

Kiru (7 ex) to put on, dress, wear.

Kiseru (7 ex) to dress, put clothes on; to cover, put over; to coat, overlay.

Kisimu (4 en) to squeak; creak.

Kisiru (6 en) to squeak, creak, grind, rasp; to clash with, disagree.

Kisou (10 en) to compete, vie, cope, contend, contest.

Kissuru (11b ex) to take, eat, drink, smoke.

Kisuru (11b en) to expect, anticipate, fix, predetermine; to attribute to, return to; to describe, record, note, write down.

Kitaeru (7 ex) to temper, forge; to drill, train, practice; to harden.

Kitaru (6 en) to come, arrive.

Kiwamaru (6 en) to end, conclude, terminate; to be carried to extreme.

Kiyomeru (7 ex) to clean, purify, clarify, consecrate, bless.

Kizamu (4 ex) to cut, chop fine, mince, hash; to carve, engrave; to notch, incise, slice.

Kidukau (10 en) to fear, apprehend, be anxious about, worry.

Kiduku (3 ex) to build, construct.

Kiduku (3 en) to notice, come to knowledge, become aware, take notice of, think of.

Kizutukeru (7 ex) to injure, wound, hurt; to defame, disparage.

Kizutuku (3 en) to get hurt, be injured, be wounded.

Kobamu (4 ex) to check, resist, oppose; to refuse, decline.

Kobiru (7 en) to flatter, fawn upon.

Koboreru (7 en) to spill, overflow, run over; to be broken, be nicked.

Kobosu (8 ex) to spill, slop, drop; to grumble about.

Kobotsu (9 ex) to break, demolish, destroy.

Koeru (7 en) to grow fat, grow corpulent; to grow fertile.

Koeru (7 ex) to pass over, go through; to exceed, surpass, excel.

Kogareru (7 en) to long, yearn after, pine for, sigh for; to be smitten with love.

Kogasu (8 ex) to burn, scorch, char.

Kogeru (7 en) to burn, scorch, singe.

Kogiru (6 ex) to cry down.

Kogitukeru (7 en) to row up to, get to.

Kogoeru (7 en) to freeze, become numb, be benumbed with cold.

Kogomu (4 en) to stoop, bend.

Kogoru (6 en) to freeze, congeal.

Kogu (2 ex) to row, pull, oar.

Kohmuru (6 en) to receive, suffer, sustain; to put on, wear.

Kohru (6 en) to freeze, congeal.

Kohzuru (7 or 11b ex) to devise, project.

Kohziru (7 en) to grow worse.

Kokasu (8 ex) to tumble, roll over.

Kokemusu (8 en) to moss.

Kokeru (7 en) to fall down, fall over, tumble; to sink, be hollowed, be emaciated.

Konomu (4 ex) to like, be fond of; to choose, prefer, delight in.

Koraeru (7 en) to bear, endure, tolerate; to retain, control, forbear; to forgive, pardon.

Korasu (8 ex) to punish, chastize, correct; to concentrate, strain.

Koriru (7 en) to profit by experience, learn a lesson.

Korobasu (8 ex) to roll, roll over, knock down.

Korobu (1 en) to roll, roll over; to fall, tumble.

Korogaru (6 en) to fall, tumble; to lie down.

Korogasu (8 ex) to roll over.

Korogeotiru (7 en) to tumble down.

Korogeru (7 en) to tumble, fall.

Korosu (8 ex) to kill, slay, murder.

Koru (6 en) to be absorbed, be devoted to; to be tasteful, be elegant.

Kosiraeru (7 ex) to make; to build; to fabricate, invent, make up.

Kosoguru (6 ex) to tickle.

Kosu (8 ex) to filter; to cross, pass, exceed, remove.

Kokimazeru (7 ex) to mix together.

Kokitukau (10 ex) to make work hard.

Kokoroeru (7 ex) to know, understand, perceive, consider, regard as.

Kokoromiru (7 ex) to try, test, assay, essay, make a trial; to tempt.

Kokorozasu (8 en) to intend, purpose, aim at.

Kokoroduku (3 en) to notice, take notice of, become aware of, perceive.

Koku (3 ex) to thresh, hackle.

Komaraseru (7 ex) to annoy, vex, bother, embarrass.

Komarasu (8 ex) to annoy, vex, bother, embarrass.

Komaru (6 en) to suffer, be afflicted, be distressed, be at a loss, be in a fix.

Komeru (7 ex) to load, charge (a gun); to include, force in, put in.

Komiiru (6 en) to be complicated, be intricate, be entangled.

Komoru (6 en) to confine oneself in, shut oneself up.

Komu (4 en) to crowd, throng.

Komu (4 ex) to load (bullet). Same as **komeru**.

Konareru (7 en) to digest; to be digested.

Konasu (8 ex) to digest; to pulverize; to belittle.

Koneru (7 ex) to knead.

Konziru (7 ex) to mix; to con- found with.

Konzuru (7 or 11b ex) to mingle.

Kosuru (6 ex) to rub, scrub.

Kotaeru (7 en) to answer, respond; to take effect.

Kotodukeru (7 ex) to entrust, charge.

Kotonaru (6 en) to differ from, vary from.

Kotowaru (6 en) to warn; to refuse; to decline; to make an excuse.

Kotoyoseru (7 en) to make an excuse of.

Kou (10 ex) to ask, beg, request, entreat.

Kowabaru (6 en) to stiffen.

Kowagaru (6 en) to fear, dread, be afraid.

Kowareru (7 en) to break, be damaged.

Kowasu (8 ex) to break, destroy, demolish.

Koyasu (8 ex) to fatten, nourish.

Kozireru (7 en) to twist, be twisted.

Koziru (7 ex) to wrench, pry.

Kubaru (6 ex) to distribute, serve out; to deliver; to allot.

Kuberu (7 ex) to put into fire.

Kubikiru (6 ex) to cut head off, behead; to discharge, dismiss.

Kubiru (6 ex) to strangle, strangulate.

Kubomu (4 en) to sink, become hollow.

Kutigomoru (6 en) to mumble, stutter.

Kutihateru (7 en) to decay completely.

Kutiru (7 en) to rot, decay.

Kudakeru (7 en) to break, be broken, go to pieces, crumble.

Kudaku (3 ex) to smash, break, crush, pulverize.

Kudaru (6 en) to come down, descend; to fall, drop; to be inferior to; to surrender, capitulate.

Kudasaru (6 ex ct. exp.) to give, condescend, vouchsafe.

Kudasu (8 ex) to lower, let fall; to degrade; to reduce, subdue.

Kudoku (3 ex) to solicit, entreat, coax, seduce.

Kuguru (6 en) to dive, to pass through; to evade, escape.

Kuihagureru (7 en) to lose one's livelihood.

Kuikiru (6 ex) to bite off, cut off with teeth.

Kuikomu (4 en) to bite in, eat into; to encroach upon; to lose part of capital.

Kuiru (7 en) to regret, feel sorry for, repent of.

Kuru (6 ex) to reel, wind.

Kurumeru (7 ex) to sum up.

Kurusimeru (7 ex) to tease, vex.

Kurusimu (4 en) to feel pain, suffer.

Kuruu (10 en) to go mad, become insane, rave.

Kuruwasu (8 ex) to make one.

Kuitaosu (8 ex) to live, at another's expense.

Kuitomeru (7 ex) to check, keep at bay.

Kuitoru (6 ex) to bite off.

Kuitukusu (8 ex) to eat up.

Kuitumeru (7 en) to be reduced to the last stage of poverty, exhaust means of living.

Kukeru (7 ex) to blind-stitch.

Kukuru (6 ex) to bundle, tie, bind; to fasten, brace; to summarize, sum up.

Kumiau (10 en) to unite, form partnership.

Kumiawaseru (7 ex) to braid, join together.

Kumikomu (4 ex) to ladle, pail, pour.

Kumisuru (11b en) to take part in, join.

Kumitateru (7 ex) to put together, frame.

Kumoraseru (7 ex) to cloud, overcast, tarnish.

Kumoru (6 en) to become cloudy, overcast.

Kumu (4 ex) to ladle, scoop; unite with, knit, plait.

Kuraberu (7 ex) compare with.

Kurasu (8 en) to pass, spend, lead a life.

Kureru (7 ex) to give.

Kureru (7 en) to grow dark, close.

Kuriageru (7 ex) to move up, carry forward.

Kurikosu (8 ex) carry over.

Kuru (11a en) to come, arrive.

Kusaru (6 en) to rot, putrefy.

Kusuberu (7 ex) to smoke, fumigate.

Kusuburu (6 en) to smoke, smoulder.

Kutugaeru (6 en) to overturn, capsize.

Kutugaesu (8 ex) to upset, overthrow.

Kuu (10 ex) to eat, feed on.

Kuwadateru (7 en) to attempt, plan.

Kuwaeru (7 ex) to add, increase; to hold in the mouth.

Kuwareru (7 en) to be eaten, be devoured.

Kuwaseru (7 ex) to feed, cheat.

Kuwawaru (6 en) to join, take part.

Kuzikeru (7 en) to be broken, be crushed; to be discouraged.

Kuziku (3 ex) to sprain, break, crush; to discourage, despirit.

Kuziru (6 ex) to pick, gore, gouge.

Kuzureru (7 en) to collapse, crumple.

Kuzusu (8 ex) to pull down, break down.

Kuyuru, same as **Kuiru**, in conjugation and meaning.

Mabiku (3 ex) to thin.

Madoromu (4 en) to dose off, drowse.

Madou (10 en) to make amends for.

Madou (10 en) to puzzle, be at a loss, be perplexed.

Madowasu (8 ex) to perplex, distract, bewitch.

Magaeru (7 ex) to imitate, mimic; to counterfeit, forge.

Magarikuneru (6 en) to wind, be crooked, meander.

Magaru (6 en) to bend, be bent, curve, swerve, twist.

Magau (10 en) to be confounded, be confused; to be mistaken for.

Magau (10 ex) same as **magaeru**.

Mageru (7 ex) to bend, curve, bow, incline; to give up, submit; to distort, twist.

Magirasu (8 ex) to continue, obscure; to divert, distract.

Magirekomu (4 en) to get mixed, be lost among other things.

Magireru (7 en) to be mistaken for, be undiscernible; to be diverted, be distracted.

Magotuku (3 en) to be perplexed, be puzzled, be bewildered, be embarrassed; to be confused.

Maiagaru (6 en) to fly high, soar.

Maikomu (4 en) to visit, call on, drop in.

Mairu (6 en) to come, go, visit; to make a pilgrimage to, pay homage to.

Mairu (6 en) to be defeated, beaten; to be dumbfounded; to be stunned, be enchanted.

Makanau (10 en) to board, provide with food.

Makareru (7 en) to be wound round.

Makarideru (7 en) to come, present oneself.

Makaseru, (7 ex) to trust a person with, give in charge of; to leave alone.

Makasu (8 ex) same as **makaseru.**

Makasu (8 ex) to defeat, beat.

Makeru (7 en) to be defeated, be beaten.

Makiagaru (6 en) to curl up, be furled.

Makiageru (7 ex) to roll up, wind up; to take away.

Makikomu (4 ex) to roll up.

Makitirasu (8 ex) to scatter about, sprinkle.

Maku (3 ex) to wind, roll, coil.

Maku (3 ex) to sow.

Maku (3 ex) to scatter about, strew.

Makuru (6 ex) to turn up, tuck; to roll up.

Mamieru (7 en) to have an audience with.

Mamireru (7 en) to be smeared with.

Mamoru (6 ex) to protect, cover; to defend, shield; to guard; to obey, observe.

Manabu (1 ex) to practice; to learn, acquire; to study.

Maneku (3 ex) to invite, ask; to bring upon oneself; to call in, beckon.

Maneru (7 ex) to imitate, mimic, ape, pretend.

Maniau (10 en) to serve the purpose; to be in time for.

Maniawasu (8 en) to make shift; to serve for the present.

Manukareru (7 en) to escape, be relieved of; to be released from, be freed from.

Marumekomu (4 ex) to juggle, cajole, coax.

Marumeru (7 ex) to make round, roll.

Masaru (6 en) to surpass, excel; to be superior to.

Maseru (7 en) to be precocious.

Masu (8 en, ex) to increase.

Matagaru (6 en) to stride, straddle.

Mataseru (7 ex) to keep a person waiting, detain.

Matasu (8 ex) same as **mataseru.**

Matiagumu (4 en) to grow tired of waiting.

Matiakasu (8 en) to wait all night, wait till dawn.

Matiawasu (8 en) to rendezvous.

Matigaeru (7 ex) to mistake, err.

Matigau (10 en) to mistake, err, blunder.

Matikamaeru (7 en) to prepare, be prepared for.

Matikogareru (7 en) to be dying for; to wait anxiously.

Matikurasu (8 en) to wait all day for.

Matikutabireru (7 en) to tire of waiting.

Matiukeru (7 en) same as **matikamaeru.**

Matiwabiru (7 en) same as **matiagumu.**

Matomaru (6 en) to be unified; to be arranged in order.

Matomeru (7 ex) to unify, systematize; to arrange, put in order.

Matu (9 en) to wait for; to expect; to treat.

Maturu (6 ex) to deify, worship; to celebrate.

Matuwaru (6 en) to be entangled.

Mau (10 en) to dance; to circle; to revolve, whirl.

Mawaru (6 en) to turn around, revolve, rotate.

Mawasu (8 ex) to turn, wheel, roll, spin; to forward.

Mayou (10 en) to be puzzled, be bewildered, be in doubt; to be infatuated; to stray from, deviate from; to be superstitious.

Mayowasu (8 ex) to puzzle, perplex, bewilder; to delude, deceive, cheat; to mislead.

Mazaru (6 en) to intermingle, be mixed with.

Mazekaesu (8 ex) to stir, confuse, disturb.

Mazeru (7 ex) to mix, mingle, blend, adulterate.

Mazieru (7 ex) to cross, exchange, interchange.

Maziru (6 en) to be mixed, be mingled, be blended.

Maziwaru (6 en) to associate with, keep company, be intimate with; to mix, mingle.

Medatu (9 en) to be conspicuous, be prominent.

Mederu (7 ex) to love, like, be fond of.

Megakeru (7 en) to aim at, point at.

Megeru (7 en) to be broken; to suffer from.

Megumu (4 en) to bud, sprout, germinate.

Megumu (4 en) to bless, favor; to give, send, present.

Megurasu (8 ex) to surround, encircle; to revolve, turn; to devise, contrive; to fence around.

Meguriau (10 en) to come across, fall in with.

Mekuru (6 ex) to turn over, turn up; to strip off.

Menareru (7 en) to be accustomed to the sight.

Mensuru (11b en) to face, border on, look on.

Menziru (7a ex) to excuse.

Mesiagaru (6 ex) to take, eat, have.

Mesitureru (7 ex) to take along with, bring.

Mesu (8 ex) to call, summon.

Metoru (6 ex) to take in marriage.

Mezameru (7 en) to wake, awaken; to come to one's senses.

Mezasu (8 ex) to seek, aim at, have in one's eye, have an eye to.

Miageru (7 ex) to look up at, raise one's eyes; to admire, respect.

Miakiru (7 ex) to be tired of seeing.

Miataru (6 ex) to find, come across.

Miawasu (8 ex) to look at each other; to postpone, put off, defer.

Midareru (7 en) to be out of order, be disarranged; to become disorganized.

Midasu (8 ex) to disturb, confuse, disarrange, derange.

Mieru (7 en) to be visible, be in sight; to seem, look, appear; to be here, come, appear.

Migaku (3 ex) to polish, rub, burnish, shine; to refine, improve, cultivate, train.

Mihakarau (10 en) to use discretion.

Miharu (6 ex) to open one's eyes wide; to watch for.

Mihazusu (8 ex) to overlook; to miss seeing.

Miidasu (8 ex) to find, catch, spy.

Miiru (6 ex) to possess; to bewitch.

Miiru (6 ex) to stare at, gaze on.

Mikaeru (6 ex) to look back, turn one's head.

Mikakeru (7 ex) to see, notice.

Mikaneru (7 ex) to be unable to bear to see.

Mikiru (6 ex) to see through; to abandon, give up.

Mikomu (4 ex) to rely upon; to expect, anticipate.

Mikosu (8 ex) to anticipate, foresee.

Mikubiru (6 ex) to undervalue, underrate, underestimate; to despise.

Mikudasu (8 ex) to look down; to despise, scorn.

Mimamoru (6 ex) to watch, gaze, stare.

Mimau (10 ex) to visit; to pay

Golden Temple

Rock Garden

a visit to.

Mimawasu (8 ex) to look around.

Minagiru (6 en) to overflow, inundate.

Minarau (10 ex) to learn, receive training; to follow another's example.

Minareru (7 en) to get used to seeing, become familiar with.

Minasu (8 en) to deem, regard, consider.

Minoru (6 en) to bear fruit; to become ripe.

Minuku (3 en) to see through.

Miokuru (6 ex) to see off, give a send-off.

Miru (7 ex) to see.

Miseru (7 ex) to show.

Misoreru (7 en) to fail to recognize.

Misuteru (7 ex) to forsake, desert, leave, give up.

Mitasu (8 ex) to fill up, impregnate with.

Mitateru (7 ex) to see off; to choose, select; to judge.

Mitibiku (3 ex) to guide, lead, direct; to usher, conduct.

Mitigaeru (7 ex) to take for, mistake for.

Mitiru (7 en) to be full of, fill, be filled with; to complete, expire.

Mitodokeru (7 ex) to ascertain; to assure, make sure.

Mitogameru (7 ex) to rebuke, find fault with.

Mitomeru (7 ex) to notice, note, observe, see, find; to recognize, perceive.

Mitoreru (7 ex) to be lost in admiration.

Mitoru (6 ex) to perceive, take in; to sketch; to nurse.

Mitugu (2 ex) to pay tribute; to support, supply with money.

Mitukaru (6 en) to be found out, be discovered.

Mitukeru (7 ex) to find out, discover.

Mitukurou (10 ex) to do at discretion.

Mitukusu (8 ex) to see all.

Mitumeru (7 ex) to gaze, stare.

Mitumoru (6 ex) to measure by the eye; to estimate, appraise.

Miukeru (7 ex) to see, observe, notice.

Miusinau (10 ex) to lose sight of.

Miwakeru (7 ex) to distinguish, discover.

Miwasureru (7 ex) to forget the face of, not to recognize.

Miwatasu (8 ex) to overlook, look over, see far, sweep, look around.

Miyaburu (6 ex) to see into, penetrate into, see through.

Miyaru (6 ex) to cast a glance, glance at.

Modoru (6 en) to return, retrace, go back; to unwind.

Modosu (8 ex) to return, put back, restore.

Moeagaru (6 en) to blaze up, flare up, kindle.

Moedasu (8 en) to begin to burn, catch fire.

Moeru (7 en) to burn, blaze.

Moetatu (9 en) to burst into flames.

Moeuturu (6 en) to spread to (fire), burn to.

Mogaku (3 en) to struggle, wiggle, writhe.

Mogeru (7 en) to be wrenched off.

Mogitoru (6 ex) to wrench from, pluck off.

Moguru (6 en) to dive, dip; to creep in.

Mohderu (7 en) to go out to worship.

Mohkaru (6 en) to profit, make profit, pay.

Mohkeru (7 ex) to make profit, gain, earn; to build, establish, set up.

Mohsiawaseru (7 en) to arrange, agree upon.

Mohsideru (7 en) to claim, demand, ask for.

Mohshikikasu (8 en) to instruct, admonish, advise.

Mohsikikeru (7 ex) to say, tell, speak, instruct.

Mohsikomu (4 en) to offer, make an offer, propose; to make application.

Mohsikosu (8 en) to send a letter, give notice, inform.

Mohsinoberu (7 en) to state.

Mohsiokureru (7 en) to neglect to say, delay in saying.

Mohsiokuru (6 ex) to send word, write a letter to.

Mohsitateru (7 en) to state, declare, allege, testify, plead.

Mohsiukeru (7 ex) to receive, accept, get, have.

Mohsiwatasu (8 en) to sentence, pronounce sentence.

Mohsu (8 en) to say, tell, speak.

Momareru (7 en) to be rubbed, be crumpled; to be trained with; to be tossed about.

Momeru (7 en) to have trouble with, dispute; to be anxious about, be uneasy.

Momiau (10 en) to jostle with, struggle together.

Momikesu (8 ex) to put out; to suppress, smother up, hush up.

Momu (4 ex) to crumple, rumple, rub; to worry about, be restless.

Monogataru (6 ex) to tell, relate, narrate.

Mononareru (7 en) to get used to.

Monosuru (11b ex) to do, make, accomplish.

Morasu (8 ex) to let leak, discharge; to reveal, divulge; to omit, miss, skip.

Morau (10 ex) to get, receive, obtain.

Moreru (7 en) to leak out, escape; to be omitted, be neglected; to be expressed, be given vent.

Moriagaru (6 en) to rise up, bulge out.

Morikaesu (8 en) to revive, rally, recover.

Moritateru (7 ex) to guard and rear; to re-establish.

Moru (6 ex) to help, serve; to heap, pile up; to administer (medicine).

Moru (6 en) to leak, ooze out, run out.

Motageru (7 ex) to uplift, lift, raise up.

Motarasu (8 ex) to bring, carry, bear.

Motareru (7 en) to lean against, recline.

Motaseru (7 ex) to give; to make a person carry; to keep, preserve.

Moteamasu (8 ex) to be unable to manage; to be worried with.

Moteasobu (1 ex) to play on, twiddle with.

Motehayasu (8 ex) to belaud, extol, praise.

Motenasu (8 ex) to treat, receive, welcome.

Moteru (7 en) to keep, last, continue; to be popular.

Motiagaru (6 en) to be lifted up, rise; to arise, break out; to happen, take place.

Motiageru (7 ex) to raise, lift, take hold.

Motiawaseru (7 ex) to happen to have, have on hand.

Motidasu (8 ex) to bring out, carry out; to propose, offer, suggest.

Motiiru (7 ex) to use, make use of, put to use; to adopt; to employ.

Motikaeru (7 ex) to shift from one hand to the other.

Motikaeru (6 ex) to carry back, bring home.

Motikakeru (7 en) to make, force, suggest, propose; to make advance.

Motikiru (6 ex) to hold out, maintain.

Motikitasu (8 ex) to bring along.

Motikomu (4 ex) to carry in, bring in, take to; to propose.

Motikosu (8 ex) to bring over, carry on.

Motikotaeru (7 en) to support, sustain, maintain.

Motikuzusu (8 en) to ruin oneself, degenerate.

Motimawaru (6 ex) to take round, hand round.

Motinaosu (8 ex) to recover, restore, revive.

Motiyoru (6 ex) to bring each his own share.

Motomeru (7 ex) to demand, claim, require; to purchase.

Motoru (6 en) to be contrary, differ from.

Motozuku (3 en) to originate in, result from; to be founded on.

Motu (9 ex) to have, take, hold, possess, carry, bear.

JAPANESE VERBS DEFINED IN ENGLISH

Motureru (7 en) to be in a tangle, be entangled, be knotted.

Mottekuru (11a ex) to bring, fetch.

Motteyuku (3 ex) to take with one, carry, bear.

Moyasu (8 ex) to burn, kindle.

Moyohsu (8 ex) to hold, give; to threaten, brew, call; to feel; to show signs of.

Moziru (6 ex) to twist, distort.

Mukaeru (7 ex) to go out to meet, welcome, greet, invite.

Mukau (10 en) to face, oppose.

Mukeru (7 ex) to turn to, direct to, bend to; to aim at, point to.

Mukiau (10 en) to be opposite, face each other.

Mukidasu (8 en) to show, lay bare.

Muku (3 en) to turn, face.

Muku (3 en) to peel, skin, strip off.

Mukuiru (7 en) to retaliate, repay, recompense, compensate.

Mukumu (4 en) to swell, become bloated.

Muragaru (6 en) to crowd, group, assemble, throng.

Mureru (7 en) to grow musty, ferment.

Musebu (1 en) to suffocate, choke.

Museru (7 en) to suffocate, choke.

Musibamu (4 en) to be eaten by worms.

Musiru (6 ex) to pluck, tear, pick.

Musu (8 ex) to steam; to foment.

Musu (8 en) to be sultry.

Musubiawasu (8 ex) to unite, join, link.

Musuboreru (7 en) to be entangled, be knotted.

Musubu (1 ex) to tie, knot, join; to bear fruit; to conclude.

Muzukaru (6 en) to fret, be peevish.

Nabiku (3 en) to bend, bow, wave; to submit.

Naburu (6 ex) to mock, banter, rally.

Nadameru (7 ex) to soothe, calm, pacify.

Nadareru (7 en) to slope to, incline to.

Naderu (7 ex) to stroke, rub, smooth.

Nagabikasu (8 ex) to protract, prolong, drag out.

Nagabiku (3 en) to take time.

Nagameru (7 ex) to see, look at, view.

Nagarederu (7 en) to flow out, run out.

Nagarekomu (4 en) to flow in, pour in, run in.

Nagareru (7 en) to flow, stream, run.

Nagaretuku (3 en) to drift to.

Nagasu (8 ex) to let run out, let flow.

Nagedasu (8 ex) to throw out.

Nagakomu (4 ex) to throw in.

Nageku (3 en) to sign, lament, moan.

Nageru (7 ex) to throw, cast, fling.

Nageutu (9 ex) to cast aside, abandon.

Nagu (2 en) to calm, lull.

Nagu (2 ex) to mow, cut down, sweep.

Naguru (6 ex) to beat, thrash.

Nagusameru (7 ex) to console, comfort, cheer.

Nagusamu (4 en) to take comfort in.

Nakasu (8 ex) to make a person cry.

Naku (3 en) to cry, weep.

Namakeru (7 en) to idle away.

Namaru (6 en) to speak corruptly.

Nameru (7 ex) to lick, lap.

Namesu (8 ex) to tan.

Naoru (6 en) to be corrected, be restored.

Naosu (8 ex) to correct, mend, repair, cure.

Naraberu (7 ex) to arrange, set in a row.

Narabu (1 en) to be arranged in a row, be set side by side.

Narasu (8 ex) to level; to ring; to tame; to accustom.

Narau (10 ex) to imitate, follow.

Nareru (7 en) to get used to.

Naru (6 en) to bear (fruit); to be completed; to become.

Naru (6 en) to sound, ring.
Natukeru (7 ex) to tame.
Natuku (3 en) to become attached, be tamed.
Nayamu (4 en) to be troubled, suffer.
Nazimu (4 en) to become familiar with.
Naziru (6 en) to rebuke.
Nebaru (6 en) to become viscid.
Nedaru (6 en) to importune, solicit.
Negau (10 ex) to beg, desire, wish.
Negiru (6 ex) to beat down the price.
Nemuru (6 en) to sleep.
Nerau (10 en) to aim at.
Neru (7 en) to sleep, lay down, go to bed.
Neru (6 ex) to knead.
Nesugiru (7 en) to sleep too much.
Nesugosu (8 en) to oversleep.
Netamu (4 en) to envy, grudge.
Netuku (3 en) to go off to sleep.
Nezikeru (7 en) to be distorted; to be perverse.
Nezireru (7 en) to be twisted, distorted.
Neziru (7 ex) to wrench, wring, twist.
Niau (10 en) to become, suit, fit, befit.
Niburu (6 en) to dull, blunt.
Nieru (7 en) to boil, be cooked.
Nigasu (8 ex) to let go, set free.
Nigedasu (8 en) to begin to run away.
Nigeru (7 en) to run away, get away, escape.
Nigirasu (8 ex) to bribe.
Nigirisimeru (7 ex) to grasp tightly, hold fast.
Nigiritubusu (8 ex) to crush in the hand; to leave unanswered.
Nigiru (6 ex) to clasp, grasp, seize.
Nigiwasu (8 ex) to make prosperous.
Nigiwau (10 en) to thrive, prosper, flourish.
Nigorasu (8 ex) to make impure, make turbid.
Nigoru (6 en) to be muddy, turbid.

Nigosu (8 ex) same as **nigorasu**.
Nikumareru (7 en) to be hated.
Nikumu (4 ex) to hate, detest.
Ninau (10 ex) to shoulder, bear.
Niou (10 en) to smell, scent.
Niowasu (8 ex) to let smell, perfume.
Niramiau (10 en) to glare at each other.
Niramu (4 ex) to glare at, stare at.
Niru (7 en) to resemble, look like.
Niru (7 ex) to boil, cook.
Niseru (7 en) to imitate, counterfeit.
Nizimu (4 en) to spread, run, blur.
Nobasu (8 ex) to stretch, lengthen; to postpone, put off; to dilute.
Noberu (7 ex) same as **nobasu**.
Noberu (7 ex) to state, relate, tell.
Nobiagaru (6 en) to stretch oneself up.
Nobiru (7 en) to extend, stretch, lengthen.
Noboru (6 en) to rise, go up.
Noboseru (7 en) to have a rush of blood to the head; to be enthusiastic.
Nobosu (8 en) same as **noboseru**.
Nogareru (7 en) to escape, get off.
Nogasu (8 ex) to let pass.
Nokeru (7 ex) to remove, put out of the way.
Nokoru (6 en) to remain, be left over.
Nokosu (8 ex) to have behind, leave over.
Noku (3 en) to move off.
Nomareru (7 en) to be swallowed.
Nomaseru (7 ex) to let drink or swallow.
Nomeru (6 en) to fall on one's face.
Nomeru (7 en) to be fit to drink.
Nomu (4 ex) to drink; to smoke.
Nonosiru (6 ex) to shout, yell; to abuse, scold.
Noridasu (8 en) to move forward.
Norikakeru (7 en) to begin to

get in; to run aground.

Norikiru (6 en) to ride past.

Norikoeru (7 en) to get over, cross over.

Norikomu (4 en) to get in, go on board.

Norikosu (8 en) to ride past.

Noriokureru (7 en) to miss (the train, car or boat).

Noritoru (6 ex) to take possession of, capture.

Noritukeru (7 en) to ride up to.

Noriuturu (6 en) to change (car, ship).

Norokeru (7 en) to brag of one's amours.

Norou (10 ex) to curse.

Noru (6 en) to ride, go aboard, mount.

Noseru (7 ex) to put on, load, take aboard.

Nosu (8 ex) same as **noseru**.

Notakuru (6 en) to wriggle, writhe.

Notamau (10 en) to be pleased to say.

Nottoru (6 en) to follow, conform to.

Nozoku (3 ex) to exclude, abolish, remove.

Nozoku (3 en) to peep through.

Nozomu (4 ex) to desire, wish, hope, expect.

Nozomu (4 en) to look over; to be present.

Nugasu (8 ex) to undress.

Nugu (2 ex) to take off, undress oneself.

Nuguu (10 ex) to wipe.

Nukaru (6 en) to make a slip (blunder); to be muddy.

Nukasu (8 en) to say (contemptuous expression); to omit, leave out.

Nukazuku (3 en) to bow, kotow.

Nukederu (7 en) to slip out, steal out.

Nukeru (7 en) to be off, slip away, come off.

Nukinderu (7 en) to excel, surpass.

Nuku (3 ex) to pull, draw, extract, remove omit, seize, capture, outrun.

Nukumaru (6 en) to become warm.

Nukumoru (6 en) to warm oneself.

Nukumeru (7 ex) to warm.

Nurasu (8 ex) to wet, dip.

Nureru (7 en) to get wet.

Nurikaeru (7 ex) to recoat, repaint.

Nuru (6 ex) to paint, lacquer, varnish.

Nurumeru (7 ex) to make less warm.

Nusumu (4 ex) to steal, rob.

Nuu (10 ex) to sew, stitch.

Obieru (7 en) to fear, be afraid of.

Obiru (7 ex) to wear, have.

Obiyakasu (8 ex) to threaten, scare, menace.

Oboeru (7 en) to learn, study; to remember.

Oboreru (7 en) to be drowned; to give oneself up to; to be addicted to.

Obosimesu (8 en) to think, consider, deem.

Obusaru (6 en) to ride on the back.

Odateru (7 ex) to instigate, incite.

Odokasu (8 ex) to threaten, menace.

Odokeru (7 en) to joke, jest.

Odorikomu (4 en) to jump into, rush into.

Odorokasu (8 ex) to surprise, startle, frighten.

Odoroku (3 en) to wonder at, marvel at.

Odoru (6 en) to jump, leap, dance.

Odosu (8 ex) to threaten, menace.

Oeru (7 en) to end, finish; to be over.

Ogamu (4 ex) to worship, adore.

Oginau (10 ex) to supply, make up, make good.

Ogoru (6 en) to be extravagant, live in luxury.

Oidasu (8 ex) to drive out, expel.

Oiharau (10 ex) to drive away.

Oikakeru (7 ex) to run after, pursue.

Oikomu (4 ex) to drive in, shut in.

Oikosu (8 ex) to outrun, outstrip.

Oimawasu (8 ex) to run after, drive around.

Oituku (3 en) to overtake, catch up.

Oitumeru (7 ex) to drive into a corner, run down.

Okasu (8 ex) to commit, perpetrate.

Okiagaru (6 en) to get up, rise.

Okikaeru (7 ex) to interchange, transpose.

Okinaoru (6 en) to sit up.

Okinaosu (8 ex) to rearrange.

Okiru (7 en) to get up, rise.

Okiwasureru (7 ex) to mislay, leave behind.

Okkakeru (7 ex) same as **oikakeru**.

Okonau (10 ex) to do, act, perform.

Okonawareru (7 en) to take place, be held; to be put in practice; to prevail.

Okorasu (8 ex) to make angry, irritate.

Okoru (6 en) to happen, occur; to be angry, become angry.

Okosu (8 en) to raise up, set upright; to wake.

Okotaru (6 en) to idle.

Oku (3 ex) to put, place, set, lay.

Okureru (7 en) to be late, be delayed, be behind.

Okuritodokeru (7 ex) to send.

Okuru (6 ex) to send, forward; to present, give.

Omoiataru (6 en) to occur to one's mind, call to mind.

Omoiau (10 en) to think of each other.

Omoiawasu (8 en) to consider together.

Omoidasu (8 en) to recollect, recall.

Omoikaesu (8 en) to think again, reconsider.

Omoikogareru (7 en) to yearn after, long for.

Omoikomu (4 en) to be strongly impressed with.

Omoimadou (10 en) to be perplexed, be at a loss.

Ooimawasu (8 en) to reflect, meditate.

Omoitodomaru (6 en) to give up, desist from, abandon.

Omoituku (3 en) to hit upon, think of, conceive.

Omoitumeru (7 en) to think earnestly of, brood over.

Omoiyaru (6 en) to enter into a person's feelings, sympathize with.

Omomuku (4 en) to go, proceed.

Omoneru (6 en) to flatter.

Omonmiru (7 en) to think, reflect.

Omonpakaru (6 en) to think on.

Omosirogaru (6 en) to be amused, be delighted.

Omou (10 en) to think of, consider.

Omowareru (7 en) to be thought, be regarded.

Omowaseru (7 en) to make (another) think.

Ononoku (3 en) to quiver, shudder, tremble.

Oreru (7 en) to break, be broken.

Oriau (10 en) to agree with, get on with.

Orikaesu (8 ex) to double, turn up, fold, repeat.

Orikasanaru (6 en) to overlap, lie one upon another.

Orikasaneru (7 ex) to fold, overlap.

Orikomu (4 ex) to turn in, tuck in.

Orimageru (7 ex) to bend, turn up.

Orimazeru (7 ex) to interweave.

Oriru (7 en) to get down, come down.

Orosu (8 ex) to take down, bring down; to drop, unload; to sell wholesale.

Oru (6 ex) to break, snap; to be, live; to weave.

Osaeru (7 ex) to press down, force down.

Osamaru (6 en) to calm down, be governed well.

Osameru (7 ex) to secure, pay, govern, rule; study, learn.

Osieru (7 en) to teach, instruct, give lesson.

Osihakaru (6 ex) to guess, conjecture.

Osiiru (6 en) to force into, intrude.

Osikakeru (7 en) to force into.

Osikomeru (7 ex) to push in, press in, squeeze in.

Osikomu (4 ex) to press in, force in.

Osimodosu (8 ex) to push back, reject.

Osimu (4 ex) to value, esteem; to regret, lament.

Osinagasu (8 ex) to wash away.

Osinokeru (7 ex) to depress, push.

Osisageru (7 ex) to depress, push down.

Osisusumu (4 en) to push on.

Ositaosu (8 ex) to push down.

Ositateru (7 ex) to hoist, set up.

Ositohsu (8 ex) to push through, carry through.

Ositukeru (7 ex) to press against; to impose upon.

Ositumaru (6 en) to be close upon.

Ositumeru (7 ex) to press in, pack tightly.

Osiwakeru (7 ex) to push apart.

Osiyaru (6 ex) to push aside.

Osiyoseru (7 en) to press on, march against.

Osoreiru (6 en) to feel small, be abashed.

Osoreru (7 en) to fear, be afraid of.

Osou (10 ex) to attack, assail, assault.

Osowareru (7 en) to be attacked.

Osu (8 ex) to push, thrust.

Osu (8 ex) to recommend, elect.

Otibureru (7 en) to be ruined, impoverished.

Otiiru (6 en) to fall, sink, run into.

Otikomu (4 en) to fall in, collapse.

Otiru (7 en) to fall down, drop down.

Otituku (3 en) to settle, reach, calm down.

Otoroeru (7 en) to become weak.

Otoru (6 en) to be inferior to.

Otosiireru (7 ex) to entice in, entrap.

Otosu (8 ex) to drop, let fall.

Otozureru (7 ex) to call, visit.

Ou (10 ex) to bear, carry; to drive away, chase.

Owareru (7 en) to be pursued.

Owaru (6 en) to end, close, be over.

Owasu (8 ex) to load, make a person bear.

Oyobosu (8 en) to affect, influence.

Oyobu (1 en) to attain, come to, extend to.

Oyogu (2 en) to swim.

Ozikeru (7 en) to fear, be afraid of.

Oziru (7 en) same as ozikeru.

-rareru (7 suff.) to be ....ed, can, be able to, be pleased to ....

-reru (7 suff.) to be, can, be able to.

Rikimu (4 en) to strain oneself, to bluster.

Sabakeru (7 en) to be disentangled, be loosed.

Sabaku (3 ex) to disentangle; to judge; to handle.

Sabireru (7 en) to be desolated, decline.

Sabiru (7 en) to rust; to age, patinate.

Sadamaru (6 en) to be settled, be decided.

Sadameru (7 ex) to decide, fix.

Saegiru (6 ex) to screen, fence.

Saeru (7 en) to be keenly cold; to be bright.

Saezuru (6 en) to sing, chirp.

Sagaru (6 en) to fall, come down, descend; to hang down.

Sagasidasu (8 ex) to find out, seek out.

Sagasimawaru (6 ex) to search about.

Sagasu (8 ex) to seek, search, hunt.

Sageru (7 ex) to hang down, to lower; to carry.

Sagesumu (4 en) to disdain, despise.

Sagewatasu (8 ex) to return, release.

Saguru (6 ex) to grope for, search, ransack, probe.

Sakaeru (7 en) to prosper, thrive, bloom.

Sakanoboru (6 en) to go upstream; to trace back.

Sakarau (10 ex) to oppose, disobey.

Sakebu (1 en) to cry out, shout.

Sakeru (7 en) to tear, rip, break; to avoid, shun.

Sakidatu (9 en) to go before, precede.

Sakinokoru (6 en) to remain in bud.

Sakinzuru (7a en) to forestall, outstrip.

Saku (3 ex) to tear, rend, split.

Saku (3 en) to flower, bloom.

Samasu (8 ex) to cool down.

Samatageru (7 ex) to obstruct, hinder, impede.

Samayou (10 en) to wander about, roam about.

Sameru (7 en) to cool, get cold; to awake; to fade away.

Sarasu (8 ex) to bleach, blanch.

Sarau (10 ex) to dredge; to carry away, kidnap; to re-learn, study.

Saru (6 ex) to leave, go away, depart.

Sasaeru (7 ex) to support, sustain.

Sasageru (7 ex) to lift up, hold up, offer.

Sasayaku (3 en) to whisper, murmur.

Saseru (7 ex) to let, make, cause.

Sasiageru (7 ex) to lift up, hold up.

Sasidasu (8 ex) to present, offer, tender.

Sashihasamu (4 ex) to insert, put in, hold.

Sasihikaeru (7 ex) to hold back.

Sasihiku (3 ex) to discount, deduct.

Sasikaeru (7 ex) to replace.

Sasikakaru (6 en) to hang over; to come near, approach.

Sasikomu (4 en) to insert, thrust in, wedge.

Sasimaneku (3 ex) to beckon.

Sasimukeru (7 ex) to direct, send, despatch.

Sasioku (3 en) to set aside, let alone.

Sasiosaeru (7 ex) to seize, attach, distrain.

Sasisemaru (6 en) to press, approach.

Sasitukaeru (7 en) to be hindered, be prevented.

Sasu (8 ex) to thrust, stab; to insert; to sting; to point out.

Sasuru (6 ex) to rub, massage.

Satoru (6 en) to apprehend, perceive; to become enlightened.

Satosu (8 ex) to admonish, advise.

Sawagasu (8 ex) to disturb, agitate.

Sawagu (2 en) to make a noise.

Sawaru (6 ex) to hinder, obstruct, hamper; to touch, feel.

Sazukaru (6 en) to receive, be given, be bestowed.

Sazukeru (7 ex) to give, impart, invest.

Sebamaru (6 en) to become narrow, contract.

Sebameru (7 ex) to narrow, reduce, contract.

Sekikomu (4 en) to be excited, be impatient; to choke with cough.

Seku (3 en) to cough; to urge, press; to hurry, be impatient.

Semaru (6 en) to be on the brink of, be near at hand.

Semeru (7 ex) to attack; to blame.

Senziru (7a ex) to boil, decoct.

Seou (10 ex) to carry on the back.

Seru (6 ex) to hasten, urge; to compete with; to bid in auction.

Siagaru (6 en) to be finished, be accomplished.

Siageru (7 ex) to finish, complete.

Sibaru (6 ex) to bind, restrict.

Sibireru (7 en) to become numb, stupefy.

Sibomu (4 en) to fade, wither, die.

Siboru (6 ex) to press, squeeze, wring.

Siburu (6 en) to be reluctant.

Sidareru (7 en) to droop, weep, hang down.

Sigeru (6 en) to thicken, grow luxuriant.

Sigureru (7 en) to drizzle.

Siharau (10 en) to pay.

Siireru (7 ex) to buy; to stock.

Shinto Temple

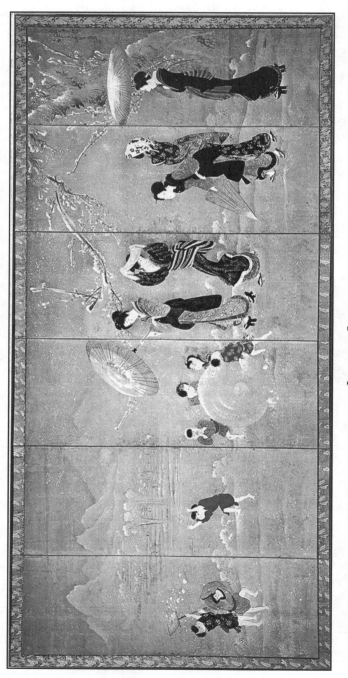

Japanese Screen

Siiru (6 ex) to force, compel; to defame.

Sikakeru (7 en) to set up, frame, challenge.

Sikameru (7 en) to wrinkle, frown.

Sikaneru (7 en) to hesitate, be reluctant.

Sikaru (6 ex) to scold, reproach.

Sikeru (7 en) to be moist, be wet.

Sikomu (4 ex) to teach, educate.

Siku (3 ex) to cover with, spread, lay.

Sikuziru (6 en) to fail, make a mistake.

Sikumu (4 ex) to design, plan, plot.

Simaru (6 en) to shut, close, be closed.

Simau (10 ex) to end, close, finish.

Simeru (7 ex) to occupy, possess; to tie up, close, lock.

Simeru (6 en) to moisten, dampen.

Simesu (8 ex) to indicate, point out, show; to moisten, dampen.

Simikomu (4 en) to soak into, sink into.

Sinabiru (7 en) to wither, wilt.

Sinareru (7 en) to be bereaved of, lose.

Sinareru (7 en) to be accustomed to do.

Sinau (10 en) to bend, be pliant.

Sinobu (1 en) to bear, endure; to conceal oneself; to think of, reflect on, yearn after.

Sinogu (2 en) to surpass, outstrip; to bear, endure.

Sinu (5 en) to die, expire.

Sinuru (11c en) to die, expire.

Sioreru (7 en) to wither, droop; to be despirited.

Siraberu (7 ex) to examine, investigate.

Siraseru (7 en) to let know, inform.

Sireru (7 en) to become known, come to light.

Sirewataru (6 en) to be known to all, be widely known.

Sirizokeru (7 ex) to refuse, reject, repel.

Sirizoku (3 en) to retreat, withdraw, fall back.

Siru (6 ex) to know, learn, understand.

Sitagau (10 en) to obey, submit to; to follow.

Sitasimu (4 en) to become familiar, become intimate.

Sitatameru (7 en) to write down.

Sitataru (6 en) to drop, drip, trickle.

Sitateru (7 ex) to make (clothes).

Sitau (10 en) to sigh for, yearn after.

Sitomeru (7 ex) to kill.

Situkeru (7 ex) to implant; to educate.

Sizumaru (6 en) to become quiet, calm down.

Sizumeru (7 ex) to sink, immerse; to subdue, pacify, suppress.

Sizumu (4 en) to sink, go down.

Sobadateru (7 ex) to prick up (ears).

Sobadatu (9 en) to stand high.

Sobieru (7 en) to rise, tower, soar, stand high.

Sodateru (7 ex) to bring up, breed, nurse.

Soeru (7 ex) to add, attach, affix, subjoin, append.

Sogeru (7 en) to split, whittle.

Sogu (2 ex) to cut off aslant, to chip.

Sokonau (10 ex) to harm, hurt, injure, spoil, ruin.

Sokoneru (7 ex) to fail, spoil, injure.

Someru (7 ex) to dye, color.

-someru (7 en) to begin to, to

Somukeru (7 en) to turn away, turn one's back to.

Somuku (3 en) to break, infringe, violate.

Sonaeru (7 ex) to offer, sacrifice, dedicate.

Sonaeru (7 en) to prepare for, provide for.

Sonawaru (6 en) to be furnished, equipped with.

Sonemu (4 ex) to envy, be jealous of.

Soranzuru (7a en) to remember, learn by heart.

Sorasu (8 ex) to curve backward.

Sorasu (8 en) to turn aside,

divert.

Sorikaeru (6 en) to warp, bend backward.

Sorou (10 en) to agree, accord, assort.

Sosiru (6 en) to slander, speak ill of.

Sosogu (2 ex) to pour over, sprinkle; rinse, wash, clean.

Sosonokasu (8 ex) to entice, allure, tempt.

Sosoru (6 ex) to incite, stimulate, excite.

Sowasu (8 ex) to marry a person to.

Soyasu (8 ex) to praise highly.

Soyogu (2 en) to breathe, fan, stir.

Suberasu (8 ex) to slip, let slip, glide, slide.

Suberu (7 ex) to reign over, control.

Suberu (6 en) to slide, glide, slip.

Subomaru (6 en) to become narrower, be contracted.

Subomeru (7 ex) to pucker, shut, make narrower.

Subomu (4 en) same as **subomaru**.

Suekaeru (7 ex) to replace, remount.

Sueru (7 ex) to set, place, put, lay.

Sueru (7 en) to rot, sour, spoil.

Sugaru (6 en) to cling to, hold on to.

Sugiru (7 en) to pass by, to go beyond, exceed, go too far.

Sugisaru (6 en) to pass, be gone.

Sugosu (8 ex) to pass, spend, exceed.

Sugureru (7 en) to surpass, excel.

Suikomu (4 ex) to inhale, breathe in.

Suitoru (6 ex) to suck up, absorb.

Suituku (3 en) to adhere to, stick fast to.

Sukareru (7 en) to be liked, be loved.

Sukasu (8 en) to leave an opening; to look through, hold to light.

Sukasu (8 ex) to cajole, coax.

Sukeru (7 ex) to help, assist.

Sukikaesu (8 ex) to plough, furrow.

Sukitohru (6 en) to be transparent.

Suku (3 en) to like, be fond of; to become thin, be empty.

Suku (3 ex) to break ground, plough, spade; to comb, card (hair).

Sukumu (4 en) to become smaller.

Sukuu (10 ex) to save, rescue; to scoop up, ladle.

Sumasu (8 en) to look wise, look composed.

Sumasu (8 ex) to finish, conclude, close.

Sumau (10 en) to live in, dwell in.

Sumikomu (4 en) to enter service, live in.

Suminareru (7 en) to become accustomed to live in.

Sumu (4 en) to live in, dwell in, reside in; to become clear; to come to an end, finish.

Suneru (7 en) to sulk, be peevish.

Sureau (10 en) to rub against each other.

Sureru (7 en) to be rubbed, be chafed.

Surikaeru (7 ex) to substitute, change secretly.

Surikireru (7 en) to wear off, be worn through.

Surikomu (4 ex) to rub in; to print in.

Surimuku (3 ex) to graze, abrade.

Suriotosu (8 ex) to scrape off, rub off.

Suritubusu (8 ex) to grind down.

Suriyoru (6 en) to sidle up, snuggle, draw near.

Suru (11b ex) to do, act, make, cost.

Suru (6 ex) to rub, chafe, grind, print; to pick pocket.

Susabu (1 en) to grow wild, increase in violence.

Susamu (4 en) same as **susabu**.

Susugu (2 ex) to wash, rinse.

Susumeru (7 ex) to promote, raise, advance, progress; to hasten; to present, offer; advise, counsel, encourage, urge; to recommend, introduce.

Susumu (4 en) to advance, march, go forward.

Susuru (6 ex) sip, suck.

Sutareru (7 en) to be disused, go out of use.

Suteoku (3 ex) to leave untouched.

Suteru (7 ex) to throw away, abandon, desert.

Suwaru (6 en) to sit, be seated.

Suzumu (4 en) to cool oneself.

Syaberu (6 ex) to chatter, prattle.

Syaburu (6 ex) to suck, lick.

Syagamu (4 en) to sit, squat.

Syakuru (6 en) to hiccough.

Syareru (7 en) to be elegant, be witty.

Syou (10 ex) to carry on one's back, to shoulder.

Tabakaru (6 ex) to cheat, deceive.

Tabaneru (7 ex) to tie up in a bundle.

Tabenareru (7 ex) to get used to eating.

Taberu (7 ex) to eat.

Tabesasu (8 ex) to feed, let eat, support.

Tabetukeru (7 ex) to get used to eating.

Tabikasanaru (6 en) to occur several times.

Tabinareru (7 en) to get used to traveling.

Tadasu (8 ex) to correct, amend, reform, adjust, question, inquire.

Tadayou (10 en) to drift, wander about.

Tadoru (6 en) to go along, trace.

Taeru (7 en) to bear, endure; to become extinct.

Taesinobu (1 en) to endure, bear patiently.

Tagaeru (7 ex) to break, violate.

-tagaru (6 suff.) to want to, wish to.

Tagau (10 en) to differ from, to break.

Tagayasu (8 ex) to cultivate, till.

Tagiru (6 en) to boil.

Taguru (6 ex) to haul in (rope).

Tairageru (7 ex) to subdue, quell.

Takaburu (6 en) to be proud, be stuck up.

Takamaru (6 en) to rise, go up, be raised.

Takameru (7 ex) to raise, elevate.

Takaru (6 en) to swarm, gather.

Takeru (6 en) to become furious.

Taku (3 ex) to boil, cook, burn.

Takumu (4 en) to invent, design, contrive.

Takuramu (4 en) to plan, devise, plot.

Takureru (7 en) to become crumpled.

Takuwaeru (7 ex) to amass, save, store.

Tamaru (6 en) to collect, accumulate.

Tamau (10 ex) to give, grant, award.

Tamerau (10 en) to hesitate.

Tameru (7 ex) to save, put away; to straighten.

Tamesu (8 ex) to try, make a trial.

Tamotu (9 ex) to possess, hold; to keep, preserve.

Tanomu (4 en) to ask, beg, request.

Tanosimu (4 ex) to take pleasure, delight, enjoy.

Taoreru (7 en) to fall, fall down.

Taosu (8 ex) to throw down, bring down.

Tarasu (8 ex) to let fall, hang down; to drop; to coax, cajole.

Tareru (7 en) to let off, hang down; to drip.

Taru (6 en) to be enough.

Tarumu (4 en) to slacken, become loose, sag.

Tasikameru (7 ex) to make sure, ascertain.

Tasinamu (4 ex) to be fond of.

Tasu (8 ex) to add.

Tasukaru (6 en) to be saved, be relieved.

Tasukeru (7 ex) to help, aid, assist.

Tataeru (7 ex) to praise.

Tatakau (10 en) to fight with, contest with.

Tatakawasu (8 ex) to fight, make a person fight.

Tatakiageru (7 ex) to train oneself.

Tatakidasu (8 ex) to turn out, drive out.

Tatakikomu (4 ex) to strike into, hammer into.

Tatakikowasu (8 ex) to knock to pieces, smash.

Tatakiokosu (8 ex) to wake a person by knocking.

Tatakiotosu (8 ex) to knock down.

Tataku (3 ex) to knock, strike, beat.

Tatamikakeru (7 ex) to press a person to do something.

Tatamikomu (4 ex) to fold in.

Tatamu (4 ex) to furl, fold up.

Tataru (6 ex) to incur a curse.

Tataseru (7 ex) to make a person stand.

Tatazumu (4 en) to stand, stop.

Tatekakeru (7 ex) to lean against.

Tatekomoru (6 en) to shut oneself up; to be surrounded by buildings.

Tatematuru (6 ex) to offer, make an offering.

Tatenaosu (8 ex) to recover one's energy.

Tateru (7 ex) to stand, erect, put up.

Tatiagaru (6 en) to stand up.

Tatiau (10 en) to attend, be present at, fight a duel, take part in a fencing match.

Tatidomaru (6 en) to stop, stand, pause.

Tatihusagaru (6 en) to stand in another's way.

Tatiiru (6 en) to enter, go into; to meddle with.

Tatikaeru (6 en) to come back, return.

Tatikawaru (6 en) to take another's place.

Tatimawaru (6 en) to move about, act.

Tatinoku (3 en) to quit, leave, move.

Tatiokureru (7 en) to be delayed in standing, lose chance at the outset.

Tatiyoru (6 en) to call on (a person), call at (a home).

Tatiyuku (3 en) to get along.

Tatoeru (7 en) to illustrate, compare, use a metaphor.

Tatu (9 en) to rise, stand up.

Tatu (9 ex) to cut, sever.

Tattobu (1 ex) to respect, honor, esteem, value.

Tawamureru (7 en) to play, sport.

Tayasu (8 ex) to cut off, eradicate.

Tayoru (6 en) to depend, rely.

Tayumu (4 en) relax, yield.

Tazirogu (2 en) to flinch, shrink back.

Tazuneru (7 ex) to seek, search, inquire.

Tazusaeru (7 ex) to carry, bring, fetch.

Tazusawaru (6 en) to be concerned in, take part in.

Tebanasu (8 ex) to quit hold of, let go.

Tegakeru (7 ex) to engage in, manage.

Tekozuru (6 en) to be puzzled, embarrassed.

Temadoru (6 en) to be delayed.

Tenareru (8 ex) to tame, train, break in.

Terau (8 ex) to shine upon, illuminate.

Tereru (7 en) to lose interest, feel awkward.

Tetudau (10 en) to help, assist.

Tigaeru (7 ex) to change, vary, alter, mistake.

Tigau (10 en) to differ from, vary, be wrong.

Tigireru (7 en) to come off, be torn off.

Tigiru (6 ex) to promise, pledge, pluck, tear off.

Tikau (10 en) to swear, vow.

Tikayoru (6 en) to approach, come near.

Tikazuku (3 en) same as tikayoru.

Tinamu (4 en) to be connected with.

Tirakaru (6 en) to be in disorder.

Tirakasu (8 ex) to scatter about, put in disorder.

Tirasu (8 ex) to scatter, dissipate.

Tiru (6 en) to scatter, disperse.

Tizimaru (6 en) to shrink, shorten, contract.

Tizimeru (7 ex) to contract, shorten.

Tizimasu (8 ex) to let contract, let shrink.

Tizimu (4 en) same as **tizimaru.**

Tizirasu (8 ex) to let curl, let frizzle up.

Tizireru (7 en) to curl, crinkle, frizzle up.

Tobasu (8 ex) to let fly, let go, scatter.

Tobiagaru (6 en) to fly, soar up, spring up.

Tobidasu (8 en) to jump out, rush out.

Tobikakaru (6 en) to spring upon, fly at.

Tobikoeru (7 en) to leap over, jump over.

Tobikomu (4 en) to jump into, rush into.

Tobikosu (8 en) to overlap, overjump.

Tobimawaru (6 en) to fly about, jump about.

Tobiokiru (6 en) to spring to one's feet.

Tobioriru (7 en) to jump down.

Tobituku (3 en) to jump at.

Tobiuturu (6 en) to flit to another thing, catch fire from sparks.

Tobokeru (7 en) to be absentminded, pretend ignorance.

Tobu (1 en) to fly, soar, leap, spring.

Todokeru (7 ex) to send, forward, deliver.

Todokohru (6 en) to be in arrears, stagnate.

Todoku (3 en) to arrive, reach, succeed.

Todomaru (6 en) to stop, stay, remain.

Todomeru (7 ex) to restrain, stop, leave.

Todorokasu (8 ex) to rumble, peal.

Todoroku (3 en) to roar, roll, peal.

Togameru (7 ex) censure, condemn, rebuke.

Togarasu (8 ex) to sharpen, point.

Togaru (6 en) to be sharp, sharpen.

Togeru (7 ex) to complete, finish, accomplish.

Togireru (7 en) to cease for a while, be interrupted.

Togu (2 ex) to grind, sharpen, polish.

Tohriawaseru (7 en) to happen to pass by.

Tohrikosu (8 en) to go beyond, pass by.

Tohrinukeru (7 en) to pass through.

Tohrisugiru (7 en) to go past.

Tohru (6 en) to pass, go through.

Tohzakaru (6 en) to go far from, get away, recede.

Tohzakeru (7 ex) to keep off at a distance, shun.

Toiawaseru (7 en) to inquire of.

Toiawasu (8 en) same as **toiawaseru.**

Toitumeru (7 en) to question closely.

Tokasu (8 ex) to melt, dissolve; to comb.

Tokeru (7 en) to melt, fuse, dissolve; to get untied, loosen.

Tokihuseru (7 ex) to defeat in argument.

Tokikikasu (8 ex) to instruct, teach.

Tokitukeru (7 ex) to persuade, solicit.

Toku (3 ex) to untie, interpret, release, disjoin; to dissolve, explain.

Tomaru (6 en) to stop, halt, end, stay, perch.

Tomeru (7 ex) to stop, turn off, hold back, detain, fasten.

Tomonau (10 en) to accompany.

Tomu (4 en) to be rich, become rich, have plenty.

Tomurau (10 en) to mourn for, condole with, attend a funeral.

Tonaeru (7 en) to recite, chant.

Tonariau (10 en) to live as a neighbor.

JAPANESE VERBS DEFINED IN ENGLISH

Toraeru (7 ex) to catch, seize, capture.
Torawareru (7 en) to be caught.
Toreru (7 en) to come off; to be able to be caught.
Toriageru (7 ex) to take up, adopt, deliver a child.
Toriatukau (10 ex) to treat, manage, handle.
Toriawaseru (5 ex) to group, combine, assort.
Toridasu (8 ex) to take out, pick out.
Torihakarau (10 ex) to manage, dispose of.
Toriireru (7 ex) to take in, bring in.
Torikaesu (8 ex) to restore, recover, bring back.
Torikakaru (6 en) to commence, begin, set about.
Torikawasu (8 ex) to exchange, interchange.
Torikesu (8 ex) to cancel, revoke.
Torikomu (4 ex) to take in.
Torikumu (4 en) to match, wrestle.
Torimatomeru (7 ex) to collect, gather, arrange.
Torimidasu (8 en) to be confused, be in disorder.
Torimotu (9 ex) to treat, entertain, intermediate.
Torimusubu (1 ex) to unite together, tie.
Torinaosu (8 en) to recover oneself.
Torinasu (8 en) to intercede.
Torinigasu (8 ex) to let escape.
Torinokeru (7 ex) to take away, remove.
Torinokosu (8 ex) to leave behind.
Torinozoku (3 ex) to take away.
Toriosaeru (7 ex) to hold back, check, arrest.
Torisaru (6 ex) to take off, remove.
Torisimaru (6 ex) to regulate, manage, control.
Torisiraberu (7 ex) to investigate, examine.
Torisizumeru (7 ex) to subdue, repress.
Torisokonau (10 ex) to miss,

lose, fail to win.
Torisoroeru (7 ex) to assort, put together.
Torisugaru (6 en) to cling to.
Toritateru (7 ex) to collect, adopt.
Toritigaeru (7 ex) to mistake, take a person for another.
Toritomeru (7 ex) to rescue, save, escape one's death.
Toritugu (2 en) to act as an agent.
Toritukeru (7 ex) to install, fit up, adapt.
Torituku (3 en) to cling to, possess.
Toritukurou (10 ex) to mend, repair, smooth.
Toritumeru (7 ex) to press urgently, persecute; to brood over.
Toriyoseru (7 ex) to get, obtain, procure.
Torokasu (8 ex) to melt, dissolve, fuse.
Torokeru (7 en) to melt, dissolve, fuse.
Toru (6 ex) to take, have, catch, get, rob, steal.
Totonoeru (7 ex) to prepare, adjust, arrange.
Totugu (2 en) to marry.
Tozikomeru (7 ex) to confine, shut in.
Tozikomoru (6 en) to confine oneself.
Toziru (7 ex) to close, shut, lock; to bind, fasten.
Tubomeru (7 ex) to pucker, shut.
Tubomu (4 en) to bud.
Tubureru (7 en) to be destroyed, fall apart.
Tuburu (6 ex) to shut (the eyes).
Tubusu (8 ex) to crush, break, destroy.
Tugaeru (7 ex) to make a pair, match.
Tugau (10 en) to pair with, be in couple.
Tugeru (7 ex) to inform, notify, tell.
Tugikomu (4 ex) to put into.
Tugitasu (8 ex) to replenish, add.
Tugu (2 ex) to join, succeed,

102

pour out.

Tugunau (10 ex) to indemnify, retrieve.

Tuieru (7 ex) to be routed, be wasted.

Tuiyasu (8 ex) to spend, expend, waste.

Tukaeru (7 en) to serve, enter service; to be obstructed.

Tukaihatasu (8 ex) to use up, exhaust.

Tukaikiru (6 ex) to wear out; to spend all.

Tukaikomu (4 ex) to embezzle.

Tukaikonasu (8 ex) to manage.

Tukainarasu (8 ex) to break in use.

Tukainareru (7 en) to be accustomed to use.

Tukamaeru (7 ex) to catch, seize, take hold of.

Tukamaru (6 en) to be caught; to hold on to.

Tukamasu (8 ex) to let grasp.

Tukamaturu (6 en) to do (polite form)

Tukamu (4 ex) to seize, grip, grasp.

Tukarasu (8 ex) to tire, make weary.

Tukarehateru (7 en) to be entirely tired, be exhausted.

Tukareru (7 en) to get tired, become fatigued; to be possessed.

Tukaru (6 en) to get into water, be soaked, be steeped.

Tukasadoru (6 ex) to officiate, take charge of.

Tukau (10 ex) to use, put to use.

Tukeagaru (6 en) to presume on, take advantage of.

Tukeiru (6 en) to take advantage of.

Tukekaeru (7 ex) to renew, replace.

Tukenarau (10 ex) to shadow, prowl after.

Tukeru (7 ex) to attach, append, affix, equip, follow.

Tukiageru (7 ex) to build up, pile up.

Tukiataru (6 en) to run against, collide with.

Tukiateru (7 ex) to run against.

Tukiau (10 en) to keep com-

pany, associate with, intercourse with; to push each other.

Tukidasu (8 ex) to push out, protrude.

Tukideru (7 en) to project, shoot out.

Tukihanasu (8 ex) to throw away.

Tukikaesu (8 ex) to push back, spurn.

Tukikakaru (6 en) to charge at.

Tukikatameru (7 ex) to strengthen, harden.

Tukimatou (10 en) to follow about, shadow.

Tukiru (7 en) to be exhausted, expire.

Tukisasu (8 ex) to thrust, pierce.

Tukisou (10 en) to attend, escort.

Tukitaosu (8 ex) to push over, knock down.

Tukitobasu (8 ex) to push away, send flying.

Tukitomeru (7 ex) to stab to death; to ascertain.

Tukkiru (6 en) to cross.

Tukkomu (4 en) to put in, thrust in, poke in.

Tuku (3 en) to adhere, gather; to take a seat; to arrive at; to possess.

Tuku (3 ex) to pound, mill; to strike, spear.

Tukurou (10 ex) to mend, repair.

Tukuru (6 ex) to make, manufacture.

Tukusu (8 en) to exhaust, consume, exert oneself.

Tumamu (4 ex) pinch, pick.

Tumaru (6 en) to be stopped up, be clogged, be choked up.

Tumazuku (3 en) to stumble over, trip.

Tumekiru (6 en) to be in constant attendance.

Tumekomu (4 ex) to cram, stuff, pack.

Tumeru (7 ex) to pinch, nip; to close, block, fill in, plug, shorten.

Tumidasu (8 ex) to send off, ship.

Tumikasaneru (7 ex) to pile up, heap.

Tumikomu (4 ex) to take on board, to ship.

Tumoru (6 en) to accumulate, estimate.

Tumu (4 en) to be pressed.

Tumu (4 ex) to pluck, pick; to pile up, heap up.

Tumugu (2 ex) to spin.

Tunagaru (6 en) to follow closely, be joined together.

Tunagu (2 ex) to tie, fasten, chain.

Tunoru (6 ex) to levy, recruit, raise, float, grow intense.

Tupparu (6 en) to push, thrust.

Turanaru (6 en) to connect, join.

Turaneru (7 ex) to link, connect.

Turanuku (3 ex) to pierce through.

Turedasu (8 ex) to take out, entice out.

Turedatu (9 ex) to accompany.

Tureru (7 en) to have a cramp; to bring with, accompany.

Turesou (10 en) to lead a married life.

Turiageru (7 ex) to pull up, hang up, fish up.

Turiau (10 en) to balance, go together.

Turu (6 ex) suspend, angle, fish, be cramped.

Tutaeru (7 en) to convey, report, impart, transmit.

Tutau (10 en) to go along, climb by.

Tutawaru (6 en) to be handed down, be transmitted, spread.

Tutomaru (6 en) to be equal to the task.

Tutomeru (7 ex) to hold a post, be employed.

Tutuku (3 ex) to poke, thrust in.

Tutumu (4 ex) to wrap, pack.

Tutusimu (4 en) to be prudent, be discreet.

Tuzukeru (7 en) to continue, go on with.

Tuzuku (3 en) to continue, follow.

Tuzumeru (7 ex) to reduce, diminish, shorten.

Tuzuru (6 ex) to spell, compose.

Ubau (10 ex) to take away, capture, snatch.

Ueru (7 en) to be hungry, famish.

Ueru (7 ex) to plant.

Ugatu (9 ex) to dig, perforate, pierce.

Ugokasu (8 ex) to move, stir, set in motion.

Ugoku (3 en) to move, stir, budge.

Ukaberu (7 ex) to float, launch.

Ukabu (1 en) to float, swim, rise to surface.

Ukagau (10 en) to ask, inquire, visit, call on, watch, peep into.

Ukareru (7 en) to give away to merriment.

Ukasareru (7 en) to be carried away.

Ukeau (10 en) to undertake, contract.

Ukemotu (9 ex) to take charge of.

Ukeou (10 ex) to contract for.

Ukeru (7 ex) to receive, accept.

Uketamawaru (6 ex) to hear, learn.

Uketoru (6 ex) to receive, accept, take.

Uketukeru (7 ex) to accept, take up.

Ukiagaru (6 en) to float up, rise to surface.

Uuku (3 en) to float, swim, come to surface.

Umarekawaru (6 en) to be reborn.

Umareru (7 en) to be born.

Umeawaseru (7 ex) to make up, make amends.

Umeku (3 en) to groan, moan.

Umeru (7 ex) to bury, inter, fill up.

Umu (4 ex) to bring forth, give birth to.

Umu (4 en) to get tired; to ripen, suppurate.

Unagasu (8 ex) to urge, press.

Unaru (6 en) to groan, moan.

Uneru (6 en) to undulate, wind around.

Uragaesu (8 ex) to turn inside out.

Uragiru (6 en) to betray.

Uramu (4 en) to hate, resent, bear a grudge.

Uranau (10 en) to divine, tell fortune.

Urayamu (4 en) to envy, be jealous.

Ureru (7 en) to sell, have a demand.

Uresigaru (6 en) to rejoice, delight.

Uriharau (10 ex) to sell off, dispose of.

Urihiromeru (7 ex) to spread by sale.

Urikireru (7 en) to be sold out.

Urikiru (6 ex) to sell out, close out.

Urikomu (4 ex) to make a sale, sell.

Urisabaku (3 ex) to sell, deal in.

Uritobasu (8 ex) to sell off.

Uriwatasu (8 ex) to sell over.

Urotaeru (7 en) to be confused.

Urotuku (3 en) to prowl about, wander about.

Uru (6 ex) to sell, deal in.

Uru (7 ex) same as eru.

Uruosu (8 ex) to moisten.

Urusagaru (6 en) to feel annoyed.

Useru (7 en) to vanish, disappear.

Usinau (10 ex) to lose, be deprived of.

Usobuku (3 en) to roar, howl.

Usuragu (2 en) to lighten, abate.

Utagau (10 en) to doubt, suspect.

Utareru (7 en) to be struck, be knocked.

Utau (10 ex) to sing, chant.

Utikomu (4 ex) to drive in, beat into.

Utikiru (6 ex) to finish, bring to a close.

Utinuku (3 ex) to punch, perforate.

Utitokeru (7 en) to be frank, be unreserved.

Utonzuru (7a ex) to be cool towards.

Uttaeru (7 en) to complain, sue, appeal.

Uttyarakasu (8 ex) to lay aside, leave alone.

Uttyaru (6 ex) to throw away, cast away.

Utu (9 ex) to strike, beat.

Uturu (6 en) to remove, move, change.

Utusu (8 ex) to remove, transfer, copy, reproduce, reflect.

Uzumaku (3 en) to eddy, whirl.

Uzumaru (6 en) to be buried.

Uzumeru (7 ex) to bury.

Uzumoreru (7 en) to be buried.

Wabiru (7 en) to apologize, beg pardon.

Wadakamaru (6 en) to be coiled.

Wakagaeru (7 en) to regain one's youth.

Wakareru (7 en) to separate, go apart.

Wakaru (6 en) to understand, comprehend.

Wakasu (8 ex) to heat to boil.

Wakeru (7 ex) to divide, part.

Wakimaeru (7 en) to understand, bear in mind.

Waku (3 en) to boil, spout, ferment.

Warau (10 en) to laugh, smile, ridicule.

Warawakasu (8 ex) to make a person laugh.

Warawaseru (7 ex) same as warawakasu.

Wareru (7 en) to crack, break.

Warikireru (7 en) to be divisible without remainder.

Waru (6 ex) to divide, separate.

Wasureru (7 ex) to forget.

Wataru (6 en) to cross over, go across, wade.

Watasu (8 ex) to take over, ferry over, span, hand over, deliver.

Wazurau (10 en) to suffer, worry oneself.

Wazurawasu (8 ex) to annoy, bother.

Yabureru (7 en) to be torn, be defeated.

Yaburu (6 ex) to tear, defeat.

Yadoru (6 ex) to lodge at, live in.

Yakeru (7 en) to burn, be discolored, be jealous.

Yaku (3 ex) to burn, scorch, fire, roast.

Yameru (7 ex) to stop, cease, discontinue.

Yamesaseru (7 ex) to refute,

confute.

Yarisokonau (10 en) to fail in, bungle.

Yaru (6 ex) to give, do, commit, perform.

Yaseru (7 en) to become thin, be emaciated.

Yasinau (10 ex) to feed, bring up, support.

Yasumaru (6 en) to be set at ease, repose.

Yasumaseru (7 ex) to give a rest, suspend.

Yasumeru (7 ex) to set at ease, repose.

Yasumu (4 en) to rest, take a rest.

Yasunziru (7a en) to be contented, rest satisfied.

Yatou (10 ex) to employ, engage.

Yawarageru (7 ex) to soften, subdue.

Yawaragu (2 en) to soften, be tempered.

Yobu (1 ex) to call, summon, invite.

Yogoreru (7 en) to become dirty.

Yogosu (8 ex) to stain, soil.

Yokeru (7 ex) to avoid, keep away.

Yokosu (8 ex) to send, forward.

Yomu (4 en) to read, recite.

Yorokobu (1 en) to be glad, rejoice of.

Yoromeku (3 en) to stagger, reel.

Yoru (6 en) to be based on, depend on, lean against, approach.

Yoru (6 ex) to choose, pick; to twist, twine.

Yoseru (7 ex) to bring near, add, collect.

Yosoou (10 en) to feign, pretend.

Yosu (8 ex) to stop, give up; to to add, bring near.

You (10 en) to get drunk, get intoxicated.

Yowarasu (8 ex) to weaken, harass.

Yowaru (6 en) to weaken.

Yowasu (8 ex) to make drunk.

Yudaneru (7 ex) to entrust.

Yudaru (6 en) to boil.

Yuderu (7 ex) to boil.

Yugamu (4 en) to warp, crook, get crooked.

Yuku (3 en) to go, come.

Yureru (7 en) to shake, quake.

Yuru (6 ex) to shake, rock, swing.

Yurumeru (7 ex) to loosen, relax.

Yurumu (4 en) to loosen, slacken.

Yurusu (8 ex) to permit, allow, forgive.

Yusuburu (6 ex) to shake, rock.

Yusuru (6 ex) to shake, rock; to extort.

Yuzuru (6 ex) to concede, yield.

Zuru (6 en) to slide, slip.

Zurukeru (7 en) to idle, procrastinate.

Japanese Writing System & Pronunciation

Written language came to Japan in the third century CE, when the Chinese ideographic script, or *kanji* was adopted. While the acquisition of a written language was a major boon to Japanese culture, the transition was a difficult one for many reasons. The primary challenge emerged from the fact that Chinese is a monosyllabic, inflected language, meaning that a single syllable can have many different meanings depending on how it is spoken. Japanese, like English, is a polysyllabic language in which inflection does not affect meaning. In addition, kanji ideograms are very complex, some being comprised of twenty strokes or more with clear standards for both stroke form and stroke order.

Because of these challenges, the written language of Japan evolved into a mixture of forms, each with a specific role in written expression. These forms are:

Kanji: The Japanese form of the Chinese written language described above. Ideograms number in the thousands, and each one is linked to an idea rather than a sound. Kanji is most often used to express place names, people's names and many other nouns, along with verb and adjective stems.

Katakaná: An angular script, katakaná is a phonetic syllabary, comprised of 46 basic characters. Each character corresponds to one sound in the Japanese language. It is most often used to express non-Japanese names, words borrowed from other languages, names of companies, and recent entrants into the Japanese language.

Hiraganá: A smoother, more flowing script, hiragana is a phonetic syllabary, like katakaná. There are 46 basic characters, each corresponding to a sound. Hiraganá shares most of the rules of katakaná and is the first writing system taught in Japanese schools. Therefore, most children's books are written in hiraganá. As students learn kanji, difficult or complex ideograms may be supplemented by hiraganá pronunciations in textbooks. Hiraganá is most often used to express simple words, verb conjugations, and particles of speech.

Katakaná and hiraganá are known collectively as *kaná*, and evolved out of the kanji system roughly five centuries after its adoption.

Romaji: Romaji is the "Romanized" version of Japanese, or the use of the Latin alphabet with which all Westerners are familiar to write out Japanese sounds. There are many systems used to make Japanese easier for Westerners to learn, including the *Kunrei-Shiki* and the *Nippon* systems. The most popular is the Hepburn system (see page 2 for a comparison of Hepburn with this text's Japanese system). While romaji will be invaluable in early study, and can be essential to business travelers or others who wish only to "get around" in Japan, students should not become too reliant on it. It is not a perfect system, and obscures some connections between words in which the same kana characters are used. In Japan, romaji appears in the popular press and in tourist information. Most Japanese have a working knowledge of romaji, can spell their names, sound out romaji words, etc.

The mix of these systems can be confusing for the beginning student, but it adds to the richness of the Japanese written language. While the two kana systems cannot be mixed in a single word, there is otherwise a great deal of freedom of expression provided by blending systems. Experienced students and native speakers will often blend systems to suit their purpose and audience.

Below are some examples of Katakaná, Hiraganá, and the corresponding Roman equivalents:

Katakaná	Hiraganá	Roman
ア	あ	a
イ	い	i
ウ	う	u
エ	え	e
オ	お	o
カ	か	ka
キ	き	ki
ク	く	ku
ケ	け	ke
コ	こ	ko
ワ	わ	wa
ラ	ら	ra

"The Actor Onoe as a Samurai Going..." by Utagawa Toyokuni

Shinkansen - Bullet Train

All You Need to Know!

Super Review®

Published by the Leader in Test Preparation

R̄EA

REA's Super Reviews Offer You—

- ✔ easy-to-grasp topic reviews which prepare you for homework, quizzes, midterms, and finals
- ✔ questions following each topic are answered with easy-to-follow explanations
- ✔ quizzes to test your knowledge of the material and guide you toward areas that need further study

Plus These Outstanding Features

- ■ student-friendly language to make learning easier
- ■ concise yet comprehensive coverage of the topic
- ■ simply presented and logically organized topic reviews

Many Different Subjects to Choose From!

ARTS/HUMANITIES
Art History
Basic Music
Classical Mythology
History of Architecture
History of Greek Art
History of Sculpture
Illustrated Bible Dictionary
Music Dictionary

BUSINESS/ACCOUNTING
Accounting
Macroeconomics
Microeconomics

LANGUAGES
English
French
French Verbs

LANGUAGES (continued)
Greek (Classical/Ancient)
Italian
Japanese for Beginners
Japanese Grammar
Japanese Verbs
Latin
Russian
Spanish
Spanish Verbs

MATHEMATICS
Algebra & Trigonometry
Calculus
Geometry
Linear Algebra
Pre-Calculus
Statistics

SCIENCES
Anatomy & Physiology
Biology
Chemistry
Entomology
Microbiology
Organic Chemistry I & II
Physics

SOCIAL SCIENCES
Psychology I & II
Sociology

COMPUTER SCIENCE
C++
Computer Networks
Java

WRITING
College & University Writing

U.S. $8.95
Canada $12.95

Visit our website at www.rea.com

ISBN 0-87891-423-4

9 780878 914234

50895